PLURIVERSE

New and Selected
Poems

Also by Ernesto Cardenal from New Directions

APOCALYPSE AND OTHER POEMS

IN CUBA

ZERO HOUR AND OTHER DOCUMENTARY POEMS

ERNESTO
CARDENAL

PLURIVERSE
New and Selected
Poems

Edited by
JONATHAN COHEN

With a Foreword by
LAWRENCE FERLINGHETTI

Translations from the Spanish by
Jonathan Cohen
Mireya Jaimes-Freyre
John Lyons
Thomas Merton
Robert Pring-Mill
Kenneth Rexroth
Donald D. Walsh

A New Directions Book

Editor's note: Grateful acknowledgment is made to astronomer Marco Lorenzi for his photograph of the Southern Cross; to publisher Alexander "Sandy" Taylor (1931–2007), co-director of Curbstone Press, for permission to reprint "The Word" from *Cosmic Canticle* by Ernesto Cardenal—with special gratitude; and to the editors and publishers of the following books and magazines in which some of the translations in this volume previously appeared: *Agni Review*; *America*; *American Poetry Review*; *Anthology of Magazine Verse & Yearbook of American Poetry*; *Apocalypse and Other Poems* by Ernesto Cardenal (New Directions); *City Lights Pocket Poets Anthology*; *City Lights Review*; *Denver Quarterly*; *Emblems of a Season of Fury* by Thomas Merton (New Directions); *From Nicaragua, With Love: Poems (1979–1986)* by Ernesto Cardenal (City Lights); *In These Times*; *Ironwood*; *Nation*; *New Catholic World*; *New Directions in Prose and Poetry*; *Pax*; *Rattapallax*; *Review: Latin American Literature and Arts*; *Street Magazine*; *Sun*; *Translation*; *Twentieth-Century Latin American Poetry*; *With Walker in Nicaragua and Other Early Poems (1949–1954)* by Ernesto Cardenal (Wesleyan); *Zero Hour and Other Documentary Poems* by Ernesto Cardenal (New Directions).

Manufactured in the United States of America
New Directions Books are printed on acid-free paper
First published as a New Directions Paperbook (NDP1127) in 2009
Published simultaneously in Canada by Penguin Books Canada Limited
Interior Design by Eileen Baumgartner

Library of Congress Cataloging-in-Publication Data
Cardenal, Ernesto.
  Pluriverse: New and Selected Poems / Ernesto Cardenal; edited by Jonathan Cohen; translations by Jonathan Cohen ... [et al.]—1st American paperback ed.
    p. cm.
  Includes bibliographical references and index.
  ISBN 978-0-8112-1809-2 (paperbook: alk. paper)
  1. Cardenal, Ernesto—Translations into English. I. Cohen, Jonathan. II. Title.
    PQ7519.C34A2 2009
    861'.64—dc22
                                    2008040582

New Directions Books are published for James Laughlin
by New Directions Publishing Corporation
80 Eighth Avenue, New York, NY 10011
www.ndpublishing.com

CONTENTS

PLURIVERSE, 1986–2005

I KNEW ERNESTO CARDENAL as a poet long before he became Minister of Culture in the Sandinista revolution. I also knew he was an early friend of the late American surrealist poet, Philip Lamantia, during his youthful Mexican sojourn.

Ernesto came to San Francisco not too long before the Sandinista uprising, and after a visit to City Lights Bookstore he wanted to find an Army/Navy surplus store. There he bought something like a half-dozen black berets. (The number of berets may have grown in my imagination, like a good fish story, but I should have surmised that a revolution was brewing.)

In the early 1980s Ernesto invited me to tour Nicaragua with him as a guest of the Sandinista regime. One of the highlights of the trip was flying with him in a Soviet-made helicopter from Managua to his hermitage on the island in Solentiname where he had created an art center to teach young uneducated Sandinistas how to paint. A whole new school of naive/primitive painting sprang up from his initiative, and the paintings became highly coveted.

This was in the early days of the Sandinista revolution, and the country was still on a war footing. One day in a military convoy with walkie-talkie communication, we set out for the Southern front, visiting a jungle training camp en route. We arrived at the Costa Rican border to find the still-smoking remains of a Sandinista outpost. (Later I documented all this in *Seven Days in Nicaragua Libre*, with photos by Chris Felver.)

Finally, Ernesto and I gave an open-air poetry reading, plus a little ceremony in which I presented to him a seed from Pasternak's grave given to me by the Russian poet Andrei Voznesensky. I don't know whether Ernesto ever planted this symbol of freedom, but he himself is such a seed.

LAWRENCE FERLINGHETTI
San Francisco, 2008

INTRODUCTION: *Songs of Heaven and Earth*

I have tried, above all, to write poetry that can be understood.
—ERNESTO CARDENAL, in conversation

E RNESTO CARDENAL is Nicaragua's preeminent poet after Rubén Darío, the leader and founder of Spanish *modernismo* at the turn of the previous century. He is a truly global poet, whose work has been translated into more than twenty languages. A Roman Catholic priest, and often called poet-priest, he is the author of numerous books of poetry, as well as prose works. Over the past six decades, he has produced an extraordinary body of verse—from epigrams to epics: poetry of love and humanity, of history and justice, and of science. In 2005, on the occasion of Cardenal's eightieth birthday, Nicaraguan President Enrique Bolaños honored him with the Order of Rubén Darío, the highest accolade in the area of culture in his homeland, for his service to Nicaragua and to humanity in the fields of art and literature. In giving the reasons for the award, Bolaños praised Cardenal for being "a man of wisdom and a firm believer in the transformation of the people and the nation through culture; a poet equally adept at epic chronicle and prophesy, who scrutinizes our past and deciphers our future." In his latest work, he has created a new, highly original poetics that integrates theories of quantum physics to contemplate the entire cosmos and the meaning of life.

Cardenal was born in 1925 in the city of Granada, Nicaragua—the colonial town the gringo filibuster William Walker nearly burned to the ground in the mid-nineteenth century—on the northern shore of Lake Nicaragua, near the volcano Mombacho. At the time of his birth, the United States had already occupied his homeland for well over a decade, and soon the guerrilla patriot, Augusto César Sandino, would lead a seven-year-long rebellion against the U.S. military presence there, fought in the mountains in the north of the country (where Sandinistas later fought U.S.-backed Contras). Cardenal's father, Rodolfo, a prosperous merchant, and his mother, Esmeralda, both descendants of colonial elites, provided him and his brother Fernando with a comfortable, upper-class life. Their home was Catholic and conservative. In 1930 the family moved to León, where Darío had lived. Cardenal felt his spirit in many ways. His great-aunt Trinidad had known the poet personally, and often spoke of him. His father read Darío's poetry to him, when he was around six years old, and although he did not understand it thoroughly, it inspired him to compose his first poem that was about Darío's great marble tomb in the Cathedral of León. Darío's famous 1904 poem, "To Roosevelt," written in response to Roosevelt's taking control of the Panama Canal Zone, anticipates Cardenal's poetry of protest against U.S. imperialism: "Hunter, the only way to approach you / is with a voice like the Bible's, or verse like Walt Whitman's." Indeed, Cardenal's future life and poetry would have a complex relationship with the United States, its people, places, culture, poetry, and politics.

The first significant phase of Cardenal's poetic development dates from roughly 1940 to 1946. The poems he composed during these years echo the major Latin American poets of the time, and he has said: "When I was eighteen, Neruda exerted the greatest influence on the poetry I was writing. . . . But the influence of Vallejo was more profound, not so much on my literary style, but on my soul." Cardenal's earliest efforts were in traditional verse forms, but by the mid-1940s he was writing in free verse with a great degree of lyricism and subjectivity. For the most part he explored themes of romantic love, often attempting to gain emotional intensity through an excess of descriptive language. His first collection, *Carmen y otros poemas* (Carmen and Other Poems), was written from 1943 to 1945, and not published until 2000 for a variety of reasons. Cardenal has described this book as "adolescent and immature."

One of the strongest efforts from the initial phase of his development is a long poem of nostalgia and disillusionment, "The Deserted City," written in 1946 just after he broke up with his girlfriend Carmen who was his first great love. It opens this way:

> Besieged by the deaths of all its afternoons forever
> on that land white as the salt on which it was founded,
> white as thirst, in the desolation of the sun
> and the death rattle of a lake that by noon feels like ash,
> dead calm, dead calm, all the way out to its horizon
> like a slab of stone fit perfectly to the infinite
> and those waves washing through an unceasing graveyard,
> often by myself I remember all the streets
> often in sleep my body has wandered through them once more
> and so at night it emerges, entirely white,
> in the midst of the land on which its ruin has been built.

Besieged by dust, by time slowly invading the stone,
a defeated city that we have to flee
because here a final ash has joined the assault
because here nothing remains and we have to leave,
we have to leave. Yet something comes back
at certain unexplainable times just after it rains
or when we sleep beneath long-absent skies
or we resume a conversation left hanging years ago,
something comes back, something can't leave for good
and so we call excitedly to some precious door
that opened in the evening to a hundred dreams of love.

Another transitional poem that should be mentioned here is "The Conquistador's Proclamation" composed the following year. This poem marks a shift from personal to historical themes, and previews a distinctive feature of his later writing, namely, poetry based on history.

The turning point in Cardenal's poetic development took place in New York. After receiving a degree in literature from the National Autonomous University of Mexico, he attended Columbia University from 1947 to 1949. There he immersed himself in the work of U.S. poets—Walt Whitman, William Carlos Williams, Kenneth Fearing, Robert Frost, Marianne Moore, Carl Sandburg, and, above all, Ezra Pound, whom he has often called his "main teacher." He began to adapt certain technical devices of these poets as he developed his own poetic style, for which he later coined the name *exteriorismo* to describe "poetry created with images from the world around us [*el mundo exterior*] . . . an objective poetry: narrative and anecdotal, made with elements from real life, with concrete things, proper names and precise details, exact dates and figures and facts and statements." It was during these formative years in New York, in the spring of 1949, that Cardenal wrote "Raleigh," his first *exteriorista* poem and, in his opinion, the earliest poem that represents his mature voice—precisely the kind of verse Pound had expected: poetry not trying "to seem forcible by rhetorical din, and luxurious riot . . . [with] fewer painted adjectives impeding the shock and stroke of it . . . austere, direct, free from emotional slither." Cardenal's later translation into Spanish of Pound's imagist manifesto, "A Few Don'ts by an Imagiste," as "Varios 'no'" would serve as a manifesto of *exteriorismo*. But Cardenal did not merely imitate imagist poetics; rather, he transformed it, and ultimately made it his own.

At Columbia Cardenal studied British and American (U.S.) literature. Among his professors were Lionel Trilling, Carl Van Doren, and Babette Deutsch. And among his classmates—unbeknownst to him at the time—was the young Allen Ginsberg, with whom he would later share a strong literary kinship and personal friendship.* Most important, in New York Cardenal began to identify himself as a poet. Although he produced only a small number of poems there, he initiated his rediscovery of the New World. The poetry that followed in the next few years would have, as Nicaraguan poet Pablo Antonio Cuadra said, "a common denominator: the vision of America from a foreign eye." Cardenal used the eye of explorers, travelers, journalists, and adventurers for recovering the wonderment and otherness of his world. And, like Pound, he adapted documentary sources, crosscutting from source to source, making a kind of verse montage that attains a lyric or epic movement of energy and whose grace lies in the cuts and seams of the poems. He continued to further develop this documentary method of writing poems, from then until now.

MANAGUA, 1950

Cardenal left New York to travel in Europe, staying for a time in Paris and Madrid, and in July 1950 returned to Nicaragua, where he settled in Managua, the capital city. He was twenty-five years old, with a growing reputation as a poet and critic. Soon after his return, he wrote "With Walker in Nicaragua." This poem is based on the history of the Filibuster War of 1855–57 and its central figure, William Walker. Known as the Grey-Eyed Man of Destiny, Walker invaded Nicaragua, made English the official language, and legalized slavery, with the grand design to attach Central America to the Slave States. Not surprisingly, he is still remembered well in Nicaragua, where schoolchildren read about his intervention and his quest for power. The poem tells the story of Walker's rise and fall from the point of view of a sympathetic old man, a filibuster in his youth, whom Cardenal created out of several different sources. In later poems he makes allusions to Walker, who personifies this chapter in the mutual history of the United States and Nicaragua, as in the revolutionary classic "Zero Hour."

"With Walker in Nicaragua" shows Cardenal's idea of love broadening. He had come to embrace his homeland, its people, culture, landscape, and history. As an expression of this love, he began to take part in the political struggle against the dynastic tyranny of Anastasio Somoza, who, as President Franklin Roosevelt once famously remarked, "may be a son of a bitch, but he's our son of a bitch." Cardenal joined a revolutionary group, and over the next few years frequently wrote articles against the government for the country's major newspaper, *La Prensa*. Despite his

---

* "What I have assimilated from Ginsberg," Cardenal explained in a 1984 interview with Kent Johnson, "is his freedom of expression; in particular his attention to the details of the everyday world. The mundane, 'un-poetic' facts of the modern world which he, more than anyone, had the vision to regard as within the realm of poetry."

growing political activity, he was still very much engaged with poetry. In early 1951, with the help of the poet José Coronel Urtecho, he realized his dream of setting up a poetry press. The press was named El Hilo Azul (The Blue Thread), and ran for a couple of years. In view of the repressive political climate in Nicaragua at the time, it was something of a revolutionary act in itself. The first book El Hilo Azul published was a translation of selected works by various U.S. poets titled *Lincoln de los poetas* (Lincoln of the Poets). Cardenal collaborated with Coronel on translating poems by Whitman, Sandburg, and others, which shared the theme of the memory of Lincoln, whom Cardenal considered the most poetic and heroic figure in U.S. history. Other El Hilo Azul books, with forewords by Cardenal, were devoted to Nicaraguan poets.

Cardenal's literary efforts grew along with his revolutionary activity. He was busy preparing a manuscript of his poems for publication, to be his first published book, but this collection never came out. Nonetheless, he was establishing himself as an important young poet. Inspired by Pound's translations from the classics, he was also translating the epigrams of Catullus and Martial, and writing his own epigrams, the earliest of which were stinging love poems. As he became more deeply involved with revolutionary politics, his epigrams became more political. For this reason they circulated in mimeographed form anonymously. Beyond Nicaragua, they were read in Mexico, Guatemala, Cuba, and Colombia, and Neruda published some in Chile, without knowing who had written them. About his epigrams, Cardenal points out: "There is more to life than revolution. There is also love. My epigrams . . . are poetry of love and hate, some of love and hate at the same time, because while they are political poems they are also love poems." The epigrams demonstrate Cardenal's increasing ability to condense complex relationships into a single, hard and clear image— again, precisely what his teacher, Pound, had practiced: "dichten = condensare." They also demonstrate Cardenal's mastery of understatement, as well as a great sense of humor that often saves his poetry from falling into rhetorical bombast. According to him, the epigrams reflect his two main passions in the early 1950s, namely, "girls and revolutionary politics."

. . .

In 1954 Cardenal's political activity culminated in his participation in an attempted revolt, later known as the April Rebellion. He had learned how to use a machine gun, and on the night of April 3, he joined an assault on the Presidential Palace. Treachery within the ranks of the rebels themselves caused the revolt to fail. Most of the leaders were captured, interrogated under torture, and killed; many others were jailed or forced into exile or they simply "disappeared" in the custody of Somoza's National Guard. Cardenal was lucky to avoid arrest, but he lived in fear of being caught. The violence he had experienced haunted him. Over the next two years he suffered a growing feeling of emptiness. He wrote more angry epigrams and the long "Zero Hour," a major section of which recounts the events of the April Rebellion. This was underground poetry, and could only be read by friends.

Cardenal came to feel that his amorous relationships with women could not satisfy him. "In reality," he later said, "my obsession with love was a hunger for an absolute, for an infinite love that human love cannot satisfy, but I did not understand this." He elaborated: "Sometimes at night, in moments of solitude, especially after a party or carousing with friends, I faced myself, and felt a hidden anguish. . . . It was as though within me I were hearing the voice of a scornful love. I was convinced God loved me and wanted me for Himself, with a jealous, tyrannical love. But I pretended to be deaf. However, the voice persisted over the years. One day I couldn't stand it anymore. I felt harassed too much by that Lover, whom I didn't love and who wanted me to love only Him, and I made up my mind to give in, to see what would happen."

The result was a great religious awakening. Toward the end of 1956 he decided to meet this "Lover." He then wrote to Our Lady of Gethsemani, the monastery in Kentucky that during his New York days he had read about in the books of the Trappist writer Thomas Merton. Cardenal was finding his way to love humanity as a whole, and to serve God. And so, in 1957, he entered the Trappist monastery at Gethsemani, where he became a disciple of Merton. Interestingly, to answer the question about his current profession when applying to the monastery, he wrote "Poet." His more recent poem, "Telescope in the Dark Night," written three and a half decades later, provides further elaboration on what its translator, John Lyons, describes as Cardenal's "apocalyptic calling to a religious vocation." In this poem, together with the modern language of astrophysics, Cardenal uses the same mystical language of St. John of the Cross, as seen in his "The Dark Night," where God is *el amado*, the beloved, the loved one, the one we might affectionately call our "love" or "lover."

Cardenal had to leave the monastery after two years, without joining the Trappist order, because of health reasons. He suffered constant headaches, and was unable to participate fully in the way of life there. He continued his religious studies in Mexico and Colombia. In 1965 he returned to Nicaragua, at the urging of Merton, and was ordained a priest. Early the next year, he founded a small contemplative commune in Solentiname, an archipelago of thirty-eight little islands located in the remote southern part of Lake Nicaragua, where less than a thousand people lived at the time. He had planned this commune with Merton, who hoped to join it, but Rome refused him the permission to do so. Cardenal named it Nuestra Señora de Solentiname (Our Lady of Solentiname). It was his calling and that of the small group of its core members, as he later explained in a famous letter to the people of Nicaragua: "Contemplation means union with God. We soon realized that this union with God was leading us to union with the very poor, forgotten peasant farmers and fishers who lived along the banks of the archipelago. This same contemplation soon led us to political engagement. Contemplation led us to the revolution. And so it had to be; otherwise, it would have been false contemplation. . . . Merton had told me that in Latin America contemplation could not be divorced from the political struggle."

The commune with its church and cultural center on the largest island, Mancarrón, became internationally known for its efforts to practice the gospel (see Cardenal's account in his *The Gospel in Solentiname*), as well as for the school of "naïve" painting that developed there with Cardenal's help. Now, through the growth of tourism in Nicaragua, Solentiname attracts visitors from around the world.

During his years in Solentiname, Cardenal's fame as a poet spread throughout Latin America and the rest of the world. He believed that his two vocations, poetry and priesthood, went hand in hand. For him, poetry had come to mean "prophesy in the Biblical sense of guidance." He published his first books, *Gethsemani, Ky.* and *Hora 0 (Zero Hour)*, in 1960, then *Epigramas (Epigrams)* and *Poemas (Poems)* in 1961. His *Salmos (Psalms)* and *Oración por Marylin Monroe y otros poemas* (Prayer for Marilyn Monroe and Other Poems) appeared in the next few years. His influential 500-page anthology of North American poetry, co-translated with Coronel, that featured contemporary U.S. poets, as well as Native American songs, appeared in 1963. The books he published after founding Our Lady of Solentiname continued to express his New World love and his commitment to the radical ideals of liberation theology: *El estrecho dudoso (The Doubtful Strait;* 1966), *Homenaje a los indios americanos* (*Homage to the American Indians;* 1969), *Canto nacional (Nicaraguan Canto;* 1973), *Oráculo sobre Managua (Oracle over Managua;* 1973), and several more anthologies offering selections of his work.

In 1977, in response to the revolutionary activities of Cardenal and members of his commune, the dictator Anastasio Somoza, Jr., destroyed Our Lady of Solentiname. He fled to Costa Rica, and became a roving ambassador of the Sandinista National Liberation Front (FSLN)—the revolutionary organization that led the Nicaraguan people to fight the forty-five-year-long Somoza tyranny. He served as a spokesman for the FSLN, which finally succeeded in toppling Somoza in 1979. His "Lights" celebrates this victory: "This revolution is fighting the darkness. / It was daybreak on July 18th. And the beginning / of all that was about to come." In that year, Cardenal was named Minister of Culture of the new government. For this government work he was suspended by the Vatican (barred from performing holy sacraments), but refusing to "abandon the people," he did not give up his position: "My job is to promote everything cultural in Nicaragua. I have a ministry of poetry, music, painting, crafts, theater, folklore and tradition, and scholarly research, which includes libraries, magazines, films, and recreation. I think of my ministry this way: just as Christ put the apostles in charge of distributing the 'loaves and fishes,' he has put me in charge of spreading culture. The people do not consume culture; they create it. This is what I did in Solentiname, only now I do it country-wide." Unfortunately, however, the Ministry of Culture was forced to close in 1988, as a consequence of the U.S.-sponsored Contra War that necessitated austerity programs leading to cutbacks in government support for the arts.

The following year Cardenal, undaunted, co-founded the Casa de los Tres Mundos (House of Three Worlds) with Austrian actor Dietmar Schönherr. This foundation and international cultural center, based in Granada, continues in many ways the cultural and educational work of the Ministry of Culture and the Solentiname commune. The philosophy of the foundation, funded through international support, is that development aid should not concentrate only on economic aspects because the causes of underdevelopment and poverty are not limited to material needs; and that only by combining material, educational, and cultural elements can a development program be effective in the long term and support sustained prosperity. The Casa de los Tres Mundos aims to serve as a connection between various traditions, and by mutual enrichment to promote awareness of the diverse cultural roots of Nicaragua. This philosophy is very much in keeping with Cardenal's vision of mobilizing the creative potential of the Nicaraguan people and rediscovering buried cultural heritage as ways to help the nation preserve its unique identity.

. . .

During the years following the Sandinista victory, the period that Cardenal was Minister of Culture, he continued to write poetry. He produced many relatively short poems, compared with his long documentary works. His new poetry celebrated the revolution and was intended to serve it: the possibility of "a society of love" in Nicaragua. His *Tocar el cielo* (Touching Heaven; 1981) and *Vuelos de victoria* (*Flights of Victory*; 1984) included victory poems, love poems, elegies to fallen Sandinistas, travel poems, ecology poems, reportage poems, as well as socially committed poems reminiscent of the agitprop written in the United States in the 1930s, such as the *New Masses* poetry of Muriel Rukeyser, Langston Hughes, and Kenneth Fearing. These were poems of history in the making, in particular, Nicaraguan and U.S. history.

In 1985 Cardenal came to New York to be the featured poet of the first Latin American Book Fair. During his stay he talked about another kind of poetry on which he was working, the poetry that forms the latest work in the present collection: "I am now writing poetry of a cosmic character, which has elements of mysticism and politics, as well as deeply personal feelings about my life, but it is framed especially in cosmologic language about the problems posed by time and space, matter, the atom, the stars and human evolution. It's likely to be long." This is the poetry of his magnum opus, *Cántico cósmico* (*Cosmic Canticle*), published in 1989. Its title suggests both the Biblical "Song of Songs" ("Canticle of Canticles") and Pound's *Cantos*, as well as "The Spiritual Canticle" of St. John of the Cross. Cardenal has described it as the culmination of his life's work of some thirty years, and further explained (with a bit of characteristic humor): "It deals with the entire cosmos. That's why the poem is so long. It is principally written in scientific language. I attempt here to unify science and poetry; also poetry and politics, science and mysticism, and mysticism and revolution." Indeed, with its epic magnificence, *Cosmic Canticle* is Cardenal's crowning achievement—a nearly 600-page poem that comprises forty-three autonomous yet integrated cantigas,* or cantos. Many of Cardenal's poems that appeared in earlier books are woven into this long poem.

John Lyons, an Irish poet now living in Brazil, who undertook the monumental task of translating *Cosmic Canticle* into English, and whose intimacy with it as its translator gives him particular insight, writes: "It would be no exaggeration to state that to Cardenal, the terms 'mystic' and 'scientist' are synonymous: in particular, the paradoxes of quantum physics with its complex simplicities are so akin to the concerns of the mystic who seeks to reconcile the impossibility of belief with the universal evidence of a God's existence and the appearance of love not only as the underlying principle but also as the ultimate purpose of evolution." Lyons's observation extends the ideas of physicist Freeman Dyson, who in his acceptance speech for the 2000 Templeton Prize for Progress in Religion said: "Science and religion are two windows that people look through, trying to understand the big universe outside, trying to understand why we are here. The two windows give different views, but they look out at the same universe. Both views are one-sided; neither is complete. Both leave out essential features of the real world." Cardenal's cosmic poetry attempts to marry these two views, and in doing so, he has created a daring new poetics and a new dimension of his *exteriorismo*.

. . .

Cardenal's life after his break with the Sandinista party needs to be considered. He was the first public figure to leave the FSLN, in 1994, publicly arguing corruption and betrayal of its revolutionary ideals in a letter published in the national newspapers. He said the FSLN had been "kidnapped by a small group" led by its General Secretary,

---

* *Cantiga*, historically, denotes a medieval Spanish song, often religious or amorous.

Daniel Ortega (today President of Nicaragua, again), whom he accused of acting like a dictator by quashing dissent within the party and cutting cynical deals with its former opponents. Cardenal claimed that the internal elections of the party were "manipulated." He added: "This is not the FSLN that we joined, for which we worked so hard nationally and internationally, for which so many martyrs died." With his break from the official party, he stopped participating actively in politics, and returned to his previous life of solitude, silence, and writing. His memoirs appeared in three volumes ("they read like novels," he says): *Vida perdida* (Lost Life; 1999), *Las ínsulas extrañas* (Strange Islands; 2002), and *La revolución perdida* (Lost Revolution; 2004).

In 2002 Cardenal came to New York as part of a reading tour in the Northeast. We gave a bilingual reading to an audience of hundreds packed into a theater at Hunter College. The white-haired poet, wearing his trademark beret, was dressed as always in a simple peasant shirt, blue jeans, and sandals despite the chill of that October night. On stage he sat on a stool behind a lectern. I stood by his side, and we alternated between Spanish and English. His reading consisted exclusively of fragments of *Cosmic Canticle*, passages taken from different cantigas to create a poetic sequence, which opened this way:

> What's in a star? We are.
> All the elements of our body and of the planet
> were once in the belly of a star.
> > We are stardust.
> 15,000,000,000 years ago we were a mass
> of hydrogen floating in space, turning slowly, dancing.
> . . . .
> we are universal,
> and after death we will help to form other stars
> and other galaxies.
> > We come from the stars, and to them we shall return.

Cardenal read his poetry with a strong lyrical voice that by the end of the reading had moved the audience to a standing ovation.

Today, Cardenal's life is one of active solitude. He lives in Managua, and works in his office at the small branch of the Casa de los Tres Mundos there. He receives visitors and entrusts a secretary, with whom he has worked since his days as Minister of Culture, with his extensive correspondence. He still sculpts, a passion that began during his student days at Columbia University. He continues to write, and gives occasional readings. He also runs a weekly poetry workshop for children with cancer at a local hospital. For all he has done, Cardenal is the nation's beloved poet, and the winner of numerous national and international poetry prizes, including the prestigious Peace Prize of the German Publishers Association for a canon that reveals "love as an essential element of social change." He is the first Latin American to receive this prize, which—the year after the 1979 Sandinista victory—he accepted not for himself, but for the great and courageous people of Nicaragua. Widely recognized as the most important living Latin American poet, he recently was nominated for the Nobel Prize.

The revered poet, though, is not revered by everyone in Nicaragua. Daniel Ortega's response to Cardenal's continued criticism of his character and politics has taken the form of a long campaign of harassment against him. In the summer of this year, it got uglier when a puppet court revived a three-year-old case, and condemned him for insulting a man over a property dispute related to Solentiname. The original charge had been dismissed in 2005; no explanation was given for its revival. In a public statement he wrote in defense of himself, Cardenal said he refuses to pay the fine levied by the "Danielista" judge, calling the sentence unjust and illegal, and that he will go to jail if necessary. Letters in support of him then began to appear daily in the Nicaraguan papers, and throughout Latin America. All protest what they see as a transparent effort by the vindictive Ortega regime to humiliate and punish him. But in the end, Cardenal will prevail—he must—because, like his poetry, he embodies the hope and heart of his country.

. . .

The present volume is the most comprehensive collection to date of Cardenal's poetry in English. He approved the selection, and participated in deciding the sequence of poems, which for the most part follows the chronology of their composition. He has a long publication history in English translation in the United States that goes back to the early 1960s, to the time of his earliest book publications in Spanish. Merton was among his first translators. He introduced Cardenal as "one of the most significant of the newly mature generation of Latin American poets" in his *Emblems of a Season of Fury*, published in 1963 by New Directions. That book of Merton's poetry includes his translations of selections from Cardenal's *Epigramas* and *Gethsemani, Ky.*, which are here in this edition. The two volumes of Cardenal's work later published by New Directions, *Apocalypse and Other Poems* (1977) and *Zero Hour and Other Documentary Poems* (1980), both edited by Donald D. Walsh with translations made by several translators, were the first to offer the full range of his poetry. These books, most of which are reproduced in the present collection, established Cardenal's reputation in the United States as a major poet.

The 1980s—the period of the U.S.-backed Contra War—saw a heightened interest in Cardenal's poetry and the publication of his *With Walker in Nicaragua and Other Early Poems, 1949–1954* (1985) and *From Nicaragua, With Love: Poems 1979–1986* (1987), both anthologies edited and translated by myself. These books are represented here. The final section comprises new poems he subsequently wrote, and, along with "Telescope in the Dark Night," includes one cantiga from *Cosmic Canticle*, "The Word," as well as two cantigas—"Pluriverse" and "3-Pound Universe"—from Cardenal's collection *Versos del pluriverso* (Verse from the Pluriverse), published in Nicaragua in 2005.

The translations in the present volume are the work of several translators from different parts of the English-speaking world. Their translation poetics vary in subtle ways, but overall they aim to convey in English a poetic "paraphrase" of Cardenal's Spanish ("translation with latitude," to quote John Dryden's famous definition, "where the author is kept in view by the translator, so as never to be lost, but his words are not so strictly followed as his sense; and that too is admitted to be amplified, but not altered"). They have brought to the task their different ears for English, for its idioms, music, and cadences, as well as their different notions of how a poem by him should sound as if he had originally written it in English. As a result, each translator has created a voice for Cardenal that may differ at times from that of the others. This is a good thing, because it allows for different ways to approach Cardenal's poetry, and because it underscores the range of possibilities of translation itself. Faithfully bringing his verses in Spanish into our Germanic tongue often requires great efforts of critical and creative ability, even when his Spanish is a translation of English. Finally, it must be noted that for this book Cardenal himself preferred just translations, rather than a bilingual format, in order to allow for the inclusion of more poems. And so, here they are—to gladden your heart and enrich your soul.

JONATHAN COHEN
New York, 2008

PLURIVERSE
New and Selected
Poems

ZERO HOUR, 1949–1959

LEÓN

I used to live in a big house by the Church of San Francisco
which had an inscription in the entrance hall saying
AVE MARIA
and red corridors of brick,
an old red-tiled roof,
and windows with rusty iron grilles,
and a large courtyard just unbearable on stuffy afternoons
with a sad clock bird singing out the hours,
and someone's pale aunt in the courtyard reciting the rosary.
In the evenings I'd hear that tolling of the Angelus
("The Angel of the Lord declared unto Mary . . .")
the hand of a distant little girl playing a note on the piano,
and the bugle from some barracks.
At night a huge red moon rose above Calvario Church.
They told me stories of souls in purgatory and ghosts.
At midnight
the shade of General Arechabala rode a horse through the streets.
And the noise of a door closing . . . A black coach . . .
An empty cart rattling as it rolled through the Calle Real.
And then all the roosters in the neighborhood crowing,
and the song of the clock bird,
and my aunt who'd leave each morning for mass at 4
with the bells ringing in San Francisco,
            ringing
in Calvario
                and in San Juan Hospital
and the jars of the milkmen clattering on the stone pavement
and a bread vendor knocking on a front door
and crying
            BREAD

                BREAD

[J. C.]

5

Due east from Peru, towards the sea, by the Equinoctial Line,
upon a white lake of salt water 200 leagues long
lies Manoa,
Manoa, mansion of the sun, mirror of the moon,
Manoa that Juan Martinez had seen one day
when at noon as he entered it they removed his blindfold
and he traveled all that day till night through the city.
I knew about it for years from reports
how it glimmers at night on the moony lake
and the splendor of the gold at noon.
All the vessels of his house, table, and kitchen, were of gold
says Gomara
and they found 52,000 marks of good silver, and 1,326,500
pesos of gold,
he says about the treasure of Atahualpa in Cuzco,
that they found 52,000 marks of good silver
and 1,326,500 pesos of gold.
For they said that the stones we brought were not gold!
And I spoke with the caciques in their houses
and gave wine to the Spaniards in Trinidad to get them talking.
And I learned about all the rivers and kingdoms;
from the East Sea to the borders of Peru,
from the Orinoco southward as far as the Amazon
and the region of María Tamball,
all the kingdoms.
And the way of life that's followed in them, and their customs.
Orenqueponi, Taparimaca, Winicapora.
It was as if I were seeing them.
The Indians along the shores, those on the islands, the Cannibals,
Cannibals of Guanipa,
the Indians called Assawai, Coaca, Aiai,
the Tuitas dwelling on trees, the Headless Ones
and the Wikiri north of the Orinoco
and the Arwaca south of the mouth of the Orinoco
and beyond them, the Cannibals
and south of them, the Amazons.
And so we set out in April

when queens of the Amazons gather at the borders
and dance naked, anointed with balsam and gold,
till the finish of that moon—
We set out in April
our ships quite a long way from us anchored at sea,
on the venture—
100 men with their bags and their supplies for a month
sleeping out in the rain
and bad weather and in the open air and in the burning sun
and plants getting stuck to their skin and the wet clothes
and the sweat of so many men together and the sun's heat—
(and I who remembered the Court)
and a sadness growing heavier by late afternoon and the buzzing from the swamps
and we'd hear monkeys at night crying filled with fear,
the scream of an animal frightened by another
and the noise of some oars,
the plash of some leaves in the river,
the step of gentle hooves upon leaves.
Voices: the sadness of those voices . . .
No prison so lonely exists in England.

And already very little bread. And not a drop of water.

Nights in cots hanging under the sky of Brazil—
that kind of bed they call "hamacas"—
hearing the current rushing in the darkness
and the drum from tribe to tribe up in the mountains
and the roar of water growing louder.

No bread. No water.
Our ears dazed by the silence.
The trees so high we couldn't feel the air.
And the roar of water growing louder.

No bread. No water.
Except for the murky water of the river, that's all.
And there's a red river that turns poisonous when the sun sets

and at night the groans of animals it sickens are heard.
And some lagoons black and thick, like tar . . .
And the heat as we drew towards the Line.
And the smell of wet leaves and the taste of weariness.
And from rapids to rapids, from cascade to cascade,
the laughter at nightfall of the green virgin of the river
and the crashing of water into water.

And the air weakening. And the jungle lonely . . .

My company beginning to lose hope.
And a day short of the land where all one desires is found!
And on the banks, flowers and ripe green fruits.
And some green birds—
we amused ourselves a good while watching them pass—
And breadfruits and monkeys and the Campana bird
and the sweet fragrance of balsam and soapberry
and the wax that the Karamana tree secretes
and the moisture in those jungles of sandalwood and camphor:
the trees were abounding in milk and honey,
they were abounding in amber and fragrant gums—
and some fruit that would burst with a bang—
from afar we'd hear it at night exploding.
And leaves big as canoes would fall upon the river.
And we saw the Crystal Mountain, we saw it afar off,
standing on the horizon like a silver church
and a river fell from its top with a terrible noise like a thousand bells.
And the daughters of the Orinoco laughing amid the trees . . .
And cascades that shone from afar like cities,
like a smoke rising over some great town
and the rumble and thunder and rebounding of the waters.
I never saw a more beautiful country:
the virgin green valleys,
the birds towards the evening singing on every tree,
the stags that came tamely to the water as to a master's whistle
and the fresh air from the east
and the glisten of gold stones in the sunlight.

Fifteen days later we sighted Guiana, to our great joy,
and a strong push of northerly wind blew that afternoon
and by night we reached a place where the river opens into three branches
and that night we lay at anchor under the stars, smelling the fragrance of Guiana.
The nearness of the land of Guiana!
But we had to head back eastward
because the rains began: those great downpours
and the rivers flooded, and endless swamps—
leaving behind Guiana with its sword of fire,
leaving Guiana to the sun, whom they worship.
And with sorrow we entered the sea once more . . .

[J. C.]

In a lonely cabin on the frontier,
I, Clinton Rollins, attempting no literary style,
pass the time by penning my memories.
And as an old man my thoughts wander back:

The things that happened fifty years ago . . .

Spanish-Americans I have known
        —whom I have grown to like . . .
And that warm, sweet, green odor of Central America.
The white houses with red-tiled roofs and with wide sunny eaves,
and a tropical courtyard with a fountain and a woman by the fountain.
And the heat making our beards grow longer.
What scenes return to my memory now!
A grey wave that comes blotting out the hills
and a muffled sound of flood waters rushing through the jungle
and the howls of monkeys on the opposite bank
and then the heavy, metallic beating of raindrops on the tin roofs
and the people running to take in the clothes from the ranch porches
and later the grey wave and the muffled sound moving off
and once again the silence . . .
And how it smelled of underbrush and the river turned leaf-green,
how the little steamboat looked there, calm as could be,
anchored to the shade of the jungle.
And the sudden flop of an iguana into the water,
the rumble of falling timber,
the distant shot of a rifle,
a Spanish word shouted from afar,
the laughter of the black women washing clothes
and a Caribbean song.

My companions on that expedition with William Walker:
Achilles Kewen, the aristocrat, who fell fighting at Rivas;
Chris Lilly, the boxer,
his throat cut while drunk one night beside a shining lagoon;
William Stoker (Bill), with his pirate's face—and a good man—
who got married there afterwards and lived by Lake Managua

(and I ate once at his house);
and Crocker, the pretty-boy,
who died gasping for breath at Rivas,
with his dirty, blond beard heavy with blood,
and one arm dangling and a half-empty revolver in the other;
Skelter, the braggart, who died of cholera;
and Dixie, the newsboy—the bugler—
who on the night Colonel Jack broke through the lines
was better than the Scottish bagpipes at Lucknow
playing his bugle.
De Brissot, Dolan, Henry, Bob Gray;
the bandit, the doubting Thomas, the bum, the treasure hunter;
the ones who were hanged from trees and left swinging
beneath the stinking black vultures and the moon
or sprawled on the plains with a lone coyote and the moon,
their rifle beside them;
or in the hot, cobbled streets filled with shouts,
or white like shells on the seashore
where the tides are always covering and uncovering them.
The ones who survived all those dangers and are even still alive.
The ones who stayed there afterwards to get married
and to live in peace in that land
and who this afternoon probably sit remembering
(thinking about how one day they might pen their memories),
and their wife who is from that land, and their grandchildren playing . . .
The ones who deserted with Turley, inland, toward the gold mines
and were surrounded by natives and perished.
The man who while sleeping fell from a boat into the water
—dreaming perhaps of battles—
and not a soul heard his cries in the darkness,
if he did cry out.
The ones who were shot by Walker against a grey church.
          And later, Walker himself, shot . . .

Hornsby had been in Nicaragua
and he spoke of its blue lakes amid blue mountains under a blue sky,
and how it was the Transit route and the great passageway,

the pier of America,
and how it would teem with merchant ships and with foreigners
speaking all tongues, waiting for the Canal;
and each ship bringing new adventurers,
and the green plantations with their great white houses with verandas;
and the planter's wife instructing the children of the blacks;
and the countryside with sawmills and palm-lined avenues humming with sugar mills
and the roads filled with blue stagecoaches
and the logs floating down the rivers.

I saw Walker for the first time in San Francisco:
I remember him as if I were seeing his blond face like a tiger's;
his grey eyes, without pupils, fixed like a blind man's,
but which expanded and flashed like gunpowder in combat,
and his skin faintly freckled, his paleness, his clergyman's ways,
his voice, colorless like his eyes, cold and sharp,
in a mouth without lips.
And a woman's voice was hardly softer than his:
that calm voice of his announcing death sentences . . .
that swept so many into the jaws of death in combat.
He never drank or smoked and he wore no uniform.
Nobody was his friend.
And I don't remember ever having seen him smile.

We set sail from San Francisco in '55.
Achilles Kewen and Bill and Crocker, Hornsby and the others:
            —on board a filibuster brig!
There were storms in Tehuantepec, and during the nights
volcanos every now and then along the coast like beacons.
In the Gulf of Fonseca, behind blue islands,
crumbling old volcanos like pyramids
seemed to be watching us:
The land where we would go through so many adventures,
where so many of us would die by fever or fighting!
And the jungle with a whistle calling, calling,
with its thick leaves like flesh, rattan palms, rushing water;
and like a constant moan . . .

No one had done us any harm, and we brought war.

When we saw Lake Nicaragua for the first time,
upon reaching the front at a bend in the road,
we halted, with a single exclamation:
               —Ometepe!
The smooth blue lake and the Island
with its two twin volcanos like breasts
joined at water level by their bases,
which looked like they were sinking in the water,
and the humble smoke rising from its villages.
And through the air's clearness
               they seemed close by.
And beneath us that glassy sand, and in the distance
the steeples of the church at Rivas.

So Rivas next and the first shots,
Walker in front on horseback like a flag.
It was noonday, and our sun-drenched clothes felt heavy on us.
Then Kewen and Crocker were wounded.
Fire! shouted Kewen
and we ran through the grey, walled street,
Crocker with his silver-plated revolver shouting.
Rivas was left filled with shouts and blood and fires burning in the sun's glare
and we returned to that blue port nestled in hills
with their curved yellow coconut palms swaying
and a small Costa Rican ship in the harbor.
There were high winds that night
with the moon swift among the silvery dark clouds.
—And De Brissot in a hospital bed, angry at Walker . . .

And in León the nights were cool
with distant guitars below wrought-iron balconies
and the wind swinging the golden lamps in front of the houses.
And as we neared the city
we heard from afar the sentries pacing back and forth
and an "alerta" one after the other running from street to street.

The voices of the people sounded strange to us
and their words ended faintly as in a song.
And the sentry's cry was as musical as a bird's in the evening.
Just the way in snow-covered small towns in the States,
come evening one hears the watchmen's voices
cheery, full and clear.
And the cry of "alerta" resounded once more.
          The girls in Nicaragua
wore rosaries with gold crosses hanging from them
and strings of pearls around their heads and black tresses.
And we fell in love with the women of that land.

One day we embarked on the *Virgin*, for Granada,
in front of those two silent volcanos like two blue guards.
The lake was glassy smooth
and all at once herons everywhere flew over the lake
as if great white flowers, toward islands where they sleep,
and flocks of screaming ducks took off in search of shelter.
At night we stopped the trembling engine in front of Granada,
and only the waves against the boat could be heard.
We covered our lanterns with canvas,
dropped anchor stealthily,
attached a cable to a tree on the shore,
and lowering some launches, we disembarked.
No one could see us advancing in the darkness with our black uniforms
          —the darkness full of fireflies and crickets—
hearing every little noise as if a big racket.
And by the time the alarm was sounded in the thick towers it was late,
as the dawn suddenly rose from the waters lighting
the foreign streets, grave and empty
of the captured town:
with filibusters in black uniform on the street corners
and our flag with its Red Star at St. Francis.

And then there was peace.
Walker spoke of peace and National Reconciliation
and kneeling with Corral in church he swore to observe the Constitution.

Granada would awake each morning with bells
and cries of vendors in the streets:

>   *I have oranges, papayas, jocotes,*
>   *watermelons, musk melons, zapotes!*
>   *—Who wants to buy?*

and water vendors with their casks crying out:

>   *Waaaaaaaater, waaaater, waaaater!*

All day long that cry of water would cool the streets
and there were stands with drinks of all colors in the streets
—some stands they call canteens there—
and processions of girls would come from the lake with their jars
and in the lake half-naked washerwomen washed laundry singing,
while men would be watering or bathing their horses.
And you'd hear the *Salve Regina* being sung through the evenings
and the air was so pure then you could hear
all the conversations of people in their doorways
and the clear serenades from afar;
and at night wet frogs used to sing in the courtyard,
or a young woman's voice behind adobe walls,
and we went to bed listening to the trickle from the clay tiles in the wet courtyard
and our thoughts would be getting mixed up
and the long rows of streetlamps were put out one after the other,
until the next day with bells again and the cries of water.

Walker in good spirits produced long cavalcades through the streets.
—But, downhearted, Corral never left his house . . .
And that day on which he was arrested (tried by court-martial,
the prisoner then threw himself on the mercy of Walker,
and Walker: that the prisoner would be shot at noon)
ladies came, with Señora Corral, and her three daughters weeping,
the youngest two embracing Walker's knees;
and he: in between officers and surrounded by his Cuban bodyguards.
And we filibusters outside listened in silence.
And that man who'd had a sweetheart in Nashville,
Helen Martin, a deaf-mute,

>   who died of yellow fever,

—for whom he learned the language of hands
and together they'd make silent signs in the air—
as if a fleeting compassion like the batting of an eyelid
had then crossed his colorless eyes of ice,
lifting his hand he said:
                    —that Corral would not be shot
at noon . . . but at two in the afternoon.
And outside we, the filibusters,
                    were hung in doubt.
And we saw the town square overshadowed by a cloud,
the still palm trees, the Cathedral, the great stone cross,
and at the end of Main Street, like a wall, the leaden lake.
And a soldier then: "Good God, how generous!"
bursting into a loud guffaw;
and he had to be taken off so he wouldn't be heard.
Corral was shot at two in the afternoon.
        Gilman gave the order:
Walker some distance away, on horseback, not taking part.
There was mourning in many houses. We heard the weeping.
And afterward there was a great calm, like the calm before a storm.

Walker proclaimed himself President
and he decreed slavery and the seizure of estates.
Meantime enemy troops we didn't see were mustering around lagoons.

The plague made its entrance with funeral drums that winter.
All was peaceful one day,
when the first volleys began to be heard drawing near
and the loud vivas on the outskirts,
and the noise of weapons and the bullets from rifles
nearer and nearer,
and the enemy moving fast in the direction of the main square.
—They'd left me behind in Granada, so I can tell the story.
Unarmed men in their homes killed in front of their families;
and a little boy murdered while eating his dinner.
Communication with the pier was cut.
—Besieged.

Patrols downstairs banging on the doors.
And from the enemy boomed laughter and guitars with bonfires during the night.
And at daybreak, there were women grief-stricken in the streets.
And then came that Englishman, C. F. Henningsen,
who'd fought against the Czar and in Spain and for the independence of Hungary.
If only we could have sailed off right then
and left that ruined Granada
       —the White Castle, as we used to call it—
with its bloodstained streets and its stinking wells full of corpses,
and the dead's grimaces lit by fires in the streets!
We protected ourselves from bullets behind piles of corpses.
Day was hot, and the air full of smoke from the fires.
And hour after hour without failing to see them,
       without failing to see enemy troops,
until night finally came
       and the rifles quieted down.
Henningsen dug trenches that night.
And the following day
the sun rose up out of the lake like an island of gold
and the shots and the whistling of bullets and the groans
let us know one more day of horror had arrived.
And we'd come to a foreign land in search of gold
and there black smoke was everywhere
and streets filled with shop goods and corpses.
All that could be heard the rest of the day were shots
and the moans of those hit by cholera,
and the calm voice of Henningsen giving encouragement.
In balconies where before girls might have been sitting
with their governesses,
now riflemen could be seen,
       with their long rifles,
and instead of polkas and waltzes, gunfire.
By the next day
the last houses on the square were burned down.
From afar the town with shooting and smoke and fireworks
looked the way it does on a holiday!

The rainy season had ended
and the fever was spreading like a fire.
At night we dumped those dead from cholera into the water
and cries could be heard from the sick who were delirious begging for water
                    —Water, water!
We threw the corpses into fires
and the acrid smoke they gave off made our eyes red
and that smoke
and the dust
and the sun on the pavement and the flames from the houses and the gunpowder
dried our mouths more
and soldiers stopped fighting to cough
and were wounded while they coughed
and dropped to the ground still coughing.
New plans were made to reach the lake
which shined at the end of the street like glass—
                                        white as ice.
We knew that many bodies were being burned.
And many groans rose from the streets during the night.
And from the outskirts, the sweet odor of the dead.
And Walker meanwhile:
            taking dips in the ocean at San Juan del Sur!
Where the blasts from the cannons did not reach
nor perhaps even our messages.

The days went by without receiving any news.
And I still relive those days in my dark nightmares.

Houses that had been familiar were no longer recognizable
and the streets could hardly be distinguished beneath the rubble:
            —a statue of the Virgin hanging by itself on a black wall.
And the ash-colored lake behind the rubble.
                    Water the color of Walker's eyes
behind the rubble
which formed odd silhouettes during the night.
And I remember a church with nothing left standing but the portico
like a triumphal arch.

And those flames spread like wildfire in the street from the lake.
And Henningsen's message was:
"Your order has been obeyed, sir:

                Granada is no more."

Help finally arrived,
with Walker himself, who stayed on the boat,
and we could make out the shots in the night from afar.
The water was still and heavy like steel
and the flashes from the rifles reflected like lightning.
And it was then that Colonel Jack, from Kentucky,
broke through the lines,
as Dixie, the newsboy, played his bugle
and in the darkness of midnight from hill to hill
that bugle shined like a glorious light
coming up to us beleaguered souls,
making the 350 who came
act like an immense army in perfect formations advancing
hitting the dirt all as one
and getting up, with their long rifles
                firing.
It was nearly two in the morning on the 14th
when all were on board.
Henningsen was the last to leave Granada.
He went into the ruined main square
and there saw around him the work that had been done;
he picked up a dead ember
and wrote on a piece of scorched hide the epitaph:

HERE WAS GRANADA

then stuck it up on a lance in the middle of the square,
and so it was.

They loved Granada like a woman.
Even today tears well up in their eyes
when they remember the loss of their dear Granada

the town of the Chamorros . . .
Where once there was love.
At last the pure waters,
the clean blue breezes of the early morning
and out of Granada with its red corpses and torches
and groans and death rattles and shouts and explosions
and the smell of the houses, rags, furniture, garbage, bodies burning!
Toward the two brother volcanos
rising out of the waters,
and through the closed-off villages
with the dogs barking . . .
And the men went back to the States.

I stayed in the country for a while, living in León.
And Bill Deshon, Shipley, Dixie, Bob Gray, Bill Stoker,
and others came to see me
and they told me about the second expedition
and Walker's death.

How on the Mississippi one night he silently weighed anchor:
They landed on the coast of Honduras late in the afternoon,
August 5,
(and most likely the 5th of August doesn't go by when they don't think back
on that march to Trujillo with a waning moon).
Dawn was coming up through the palms
when they arrived
to the sharp cry of the sentries
at the fort with stained ramparts and silvery cannons.
And they took the fort.
The houses were made of stone, with one floor, and red-tiled roofs
held up by cane poles on top of big beams,
and many big iguanas on the roofs.

It was there that Henry,
drunk, smoking a cigar near the gunpowder,
was shot by Dolan, the bullet hitting him
right in the mouth,

and Walker came quick to gather him up,
as Dolan was explaining how it happened.
And so Walker sat down at Henry's bedside,
and the sun went down, the moon rose
and he was still there
and the whole night went by
and he was still there,
applying wet cloths to Henry's wounded face,
and in the morning he left, and relieved the guards.
Dolan spoke of reinforcements
                    but they never did come.
And then came the ultimatum from the British.
Walker entered once more and sat down at Henry's bedside.
Henry couldn't speak, so he had a slate on which he wrote.
Walker took the slate and wrote a few words
and handed him the slate.
Henry was thinking hard.
Then he took the slate and wrote a single word.
Walker glanced at the slate.
He sat still a long time thinking,
                    then left.
Worms had eaten away half of his face.
On a table beside his bed was a bottle marked
                    "morphine"
and part of a glass of green lemonade.
And when Walker left, he sat up,
put a few spoonfuls from the bottle into the glass,
stirred it up a little and drank it,
lay down again,
pulled the thin blanket carefully over himself,
folded his hands on his chest
and went to sleep.
          And he never woke up.
It was midnight when Dolan came in.
He glanced at Henry and went over,
looked at the slate, read the word,
and said:

"that explains it."
Then they marched out in ranks,
each with a blanket and rifle,
in search of Cabañas' camp,
because that had been Henry's word: "Cabañas."
They went through a grove of orange trees.
They marched swiftly and in silence all night,
without stopping to bury their dead.
They halted in the evening for the moon to rise
and a guard was posted.
They marched more by night.
They halted at sunrise
at a banana plantation.
Bullets were bursting from the leaves.
They fired back at them when they stopped to drink,
                        behind banana trees.
Walker was wounded slightly on one cheek
(the first bullet to wound him in a battle).
And they finally reached Cabañas' camp
and found the rifle pits but no Cabañas.
What long, hot days those were
in sticky swamps with heavy rifles
from dawn until the blood-red sundowns hot as hell!

Walker with fever, paler than ever.

And they lost all track of the days.
Until one day they saw the British coming up the river.
General Walker was the last to climb aboard.
                        —All that are alive, sir!
It was daylight when they woke up, at anchor at Trujillo,
and it looked like a grimace hung above the black fort.
And they put the wounded under sailcloth awnings.

In the fort they were court-martialing Walker.
They saw him pass by the next morning surrounded by guards,
his face pale as always,

and they could see the scar, paler, on his cheek.
He carried a crucifix in his hand.

When they halted
the officer commanding the guard
read a paper in Spanish,
            surely his orders.
And then Walker, in a calm and dignified voice,
without trembling,
spoke in Spanish.
And the filibusters didn't hear what he said.
They could see from where they stood
a newly made grave in the sand,
and Walker, who kept speaking, calm and dignified,
            beside the grave.
And the man said:
            "The President
the President of Nicaragua, is a Nicaraguan . . ."
There was a drum roll
and gunfire.
All the bullets hit the mark.
Out of ninety-one men only twelve made it back.
And there, by the sea, with no wreaths or epitaph remained
William Walker of Tennessee.

[J. C.]

THE FILIBUSTERS

There were scoundrels, thieves, gamblers, gunslingers.
There were also honest men and gentlemen and brave men.
Fellows enlisting out of necessity and illusions:
Some fellow out of work one morning would be on a pier,
and an agent of Walker would come up with a free passage
to Nicaragua.
                    —Toward where there was no passage back.
Or they came for 160 acres of land in Central America
(to sell it) and 25 bucks a month,
and they fought for nothing a month, and six square feet of earth.
Or they'd come in search of glory: a name
forever written down in the pages of History.
And their names were forgotten,
in barracks with boards taken out to make their coffins
and the drunken sergeant, pigs, crap;
or in those hospitals consisting of mango, coconut, and almond groves
where they grew delirious surrounded by howler monkeys and magpies,
getting chills from the wind off the Lake.
And the luckiest ones were those who died in battles
or in ambushes at night along strange roads like a dream,
or by accidents or sudden death.
And always loaded with more filibusters
and more filibusters,
bound for San Juan del Sur
                    and for San Juan del Norte,
the "Transit Company" would come
                    like Charon's boat.
Vanderbilt and Morgan knew where we were going
                    (almost all died)
and down in Nicaragua they stole money from the dead.

                                                    [J. C.]

24

JOSÉ DOLORES ESTRADA

To all Nicaraguans in exile

He fought against the Spanish governor in the streets of Xalteva
in the unsuccessful rebellion of April 1812.
But the glory wasn't his. He was a boy then,
and other rebels were the leaders.
He later defeated the Yankees at the San Jacinto ranch.
He was general then. But the glory wasn't just his.
Soldiers and peasants fought, too.
Now an old man in exile for opposing the re-election
of the President (his close friend)
he writes to his friends from Costa Rica:

I am clearing a little patch here
to see if I can grow some tobacco plants.

And that was his great glory:
because it was his hardest battle, and the one in which he fought alone,
with no general, or soldiers, or trumpets, or victory.

[J. C.]

Green afternoons in the jungle; sad
afternoons. A green river
flowing through green pastures;
green marshes.
Afternoons that smell of mud, rain-soaked leaves, of
wet ferns and mushrooms.
The green, moss-covered sloth
little by little climbing from branch to
branch, with its eyes closed as if
asleep but eating
a leaf, stretching out one front claw
followed by the other,
not bothered at all by the ants biting it,
slowly turning its round funny-looking
face, first to one side
and then the other,
finally wrapping its tail around a branch
and hanging down heavily like
a ball of lead;
the shad leaping in the river;
the din of monkeys eating
ill-manneredly, quick as they can,
throwing soursop peels at each other
and fighting, chattering, mimicking one another
and laughing in the trees;
screeching female monkeys carrying pickaback
bald babies with lips flared;
the elastic long-whiskered agouti
that stretches and shrinks up
looking all around with its round eyes
while it eats, trembling;
spiny iguanas
like jade dragons
shooting over the water
(jade arrows!);
the black man with his striped shirt, paddling
in his ceiba canoe.

A girl swinging back and forth in a hammock,
with long black hair, and a bare leg
hanging out of the hammock,
greets us:

> *Adios, California!*

The black river, like ink, at dusk.
Some flower with a sickening stench

> like a corpse;

and a horrible flower, all hairy.

> Orchids

hanging over stagnant water.
Sad whistles in the jungle,
and moans.

> Moans.

Sad leaves that fall spinning around.
And screeches . . .

> A cry among the *guanabanas*!

An ax chopping a log

> and the echo of the ax.

The same screeching!
Packs of wild pigs grunting.
Outbursts of laughter!

> The song of a toucan.

Rattling of rattlesnakes.
Cries of howler monkeys.

> *Chachalacas.*

The melancholy song of the *gongolona*

> among coquito palms,

and the song of the dove "go-go-lay,

> go-go-lay, go-lay, go-lay."

Songful golden orioles
swaying in their nests suspended from palm trees,
and the song of the lion bird in the cohune palms
and the song of the moon-and-sun bird
and the bugler bird, the clock
bird singing out the hour

and the potoo that sings at night (oh poor me)
>   "Poor-me-one"   "Poor-me-one"
pairs of macaws that pass by squawking,
and the *güis, chichitote* and "feeling-joy"
>   "feeling-joyyyyyyy"
which they sing in among the gloomy bogs.
Silvery marshes all aglow,
and the frogs singing
>   "rrrrrrrrrrrrr"
And a bird that all night keeps calling its name!

The sun setting behind Orosi: Orosi
rose-colored, the sky crimson, and the fiery Archipelago
of the Solentinames, floating in liquid gold,
and the lake then rose-colored, and then opal, and the green
palm trees on the islands against the sky,
and the sky then grey, and the water grey;
and a sad star shines in the evening sky.
The oarsmen sing:
>   *Ave Maria purisima . . .*
and then a silence;
>   just
the waves of the lake in the peaceful night.
>   The moon above the lake
and the silhouette of dark palms in the moonlight.

Just the water beating against our bungo.

The island of Ometepe: the water green below the island.
In the water a launch leaning with its sails rolled up.
On the island, clothes of every color spread out on the beach.
A cart with its oxen drinking water.
A naked boy bathing his horse.
And Indians (quite short) carrying firewood.
Behind grey huts.
Gold-colored coconuts.
And up above the green volcano

blowing out a lazy puff of smoke
                    into the blue air.

The blue lake.
The white heron.
                    And a white sail in the distance.

Green islets, with black rocks and
icacos, plantain groves, palms, and papayas,
and cane huts among the plantain groves.
                                        Where
the yellow bellflowers of the "gloria de Nicaragua"
hanging from trees
and trailing over rocks
                    sway above the water.
And in that mirror of water
upside down, the green islets
with their black rocks and their icacos
plantain groves, palms, and papayas.
A black boat lashed to the shore;
in the water a woman with bare breasts
and a purple skirt,
washing clothes on a white rock,
the water up to her knees;
and her long straight hair falling freely to the water;
and her purple skirt,
bare breasts,
black hair,
black boat,
            reflected in the water.
And far off
the silhouette of a boat with two people
                    rounding an island.

The first night in Granada: Granada
under siege; and throughout the night
every 2 minutes they shouted *Alerta!*

(And that night I dreamt of storms on the lake.
Iguanas walking over Rio Frio
and the sailors were singing the Salve
and Bernabe Somoza was attacking Granada . . .)
On the tiled roofs of Granada
that dazzling verdure:
                    —like a fire burning green.
And the first streetlamps
            pale, in the twilight.
A polka on a distant piano.
And amid the smell of narcissus
a song rises from a courtyard:
                    Delgadina, get up and
                    put on your white dress.
And a peal of bells
            clear and harsh
            and clear and clear
                    (cling-clang, cling-clang)
a harsh iron sound alternating with clear iron sounds:
                            —it's the tolling of the Angelus!

Nindirí!
How shall I describe you,
Nindirí,
beautiful Nindirí!
Beneath green vaults:
avenues; the smooth
avenues of Nindirí.
Simple huts made out of cane
under the green branches,
like nests.
Nindirí:
the musical name which they gave you
when Rome was still young.
(*Neenda*, water; and *Diria*, mountain)
tells us in an ancient, forgotten tongue
of the lake and the volcano.

Nindirí, beautiful Nindirí:
oranges, golden bananas, icaco plums,
gold among the leaves.
Girls the color of chocolate,
their breasts bare,
spinning white cotton among the trees.
Quiet primitive Nindirí,
seat of the ancient caciques and their courts,
—vision of the night, some dreamy Arcadia,
unreal!
How shall I forget you!
That small lake in the crater, as if in a goblet,
and the women washing clothes in the lake.
The lava: like a sea of molten iron,
a sea of red rock, treeless,
a storm turned to stone, swirls, waves
upon waves, knife-sharp.

White and light purple hyacinths on the farms;
and the flower of the *malinche*, the *sacuanjoche*
flower,
in their curls and braids black as jet.
Smiles on lips rouged with annatto.
And the girls of Masaya,
with their large red earthen jars and pots
            and their white sleeveless blouses.

—Straight as grenadiers
            under the water jars . . .

            And with no more covering
than the foam and rose-colored water,
splashing water on themselves with gourds,
and their hair floating in the water . . .

Mandolins and moonlight on balconies.
Marimbas. Marimbas of Monimbó.

A lagoon silver-looking in the moonlight!

And those dark-skinned women of Nindirí
smiling in the doorways of their huts would greet
the passing traveler:
                Adios, Americano!

Cloudy grey dawns
smelling of milk and fresh manure and dried hay
with the lowing of cows and young calves,
and a native grackle—the *zanate*—singing on a cow.
Dry huts, smoking, in the dry countryside.
Or wet huts, green rain-soaked grass,
and white houses with red-tiled roofs drenched
under the light blue sky.
Pale fireflies around evening time
and the sad cicada,
cicadas,
and the cart
and the song of the cart driver.
And the *zanate* singing on a fence.

Good-bye, Gentlemen
                Have a good trip, Sir

On the roads there was always a cross
with dried flowers . . .

And the tiny light in the brush, and the barking far off.
And fires far off in the hills.

A bell heard from behind the ceiba trees
with a piercing sound:
        It's the hour for Vespers
                and we are near Managua.

The girls of Managua

toward evening would go singing down to the lake shore
to fill their water jars.

        Silvery sardines were leaping up in the water.

Noon by Lake Managua:
The smoke from Momotombo hanging in the sky.
A buzzard stopped in the middle of its flight.
And the sun shining down without casting a shadow.

The two girls of Buena Vista:
      "The white one" and "the black one."
        Buena Vees-ta, Gentlemen!
This here farm is called Santa Maria de Buena Vista!
These are my little boys
and those my big girls!
One was white with light hair and blue eyes
      and the other dark-skinned.
        The black one is my husband's daughter
          and the other one a Frenchman's!
And green parrots in the trees.
A cane hut
surrounded by palm and plantain trees.
        Gentlemen, I was young once . . .
And two little heads together sticking out of the doorway;
the kids naked, frightened.
Good-bye, sweethearts!
        God preserve you, Gentlemen!
"Califooooooornia?"

Even rows of palm trees
and at the end of the cane fields
a red roof.
The blue steam from the mill,
the smell of sugar-cane juice,
        and a hammock swinging back and forth.
A monotonous mill
      about to stop at each turn.

In the sun, a cart loaded with firewood,
being pulled by two sleepy oxen.

            Giddyap, giddyap you bastard.
On the wall, a rifle,
a portrait of Lola Montez,
and a tiger skin.
And in the air, the flight of a fly like a thread.
Buzzards circling in the sky.
And the hammock swinging back and forth.

       And that drowsy milling of sugar cane.
Giddyap Canelo.

A green cross by a spring-fed pool,
decorated with dried wreaths,
and a little boy sitting at the foot of the cross.
And so I asked him why that cross was there:
It's to recall a horrible crime, he told me.
And I learned nothing else about the cross,
except that the victim was a woman.

[J. C.]

Above the rain-soaked track down which the girls with their jars
come and go,
       on steps cut in the rock,
from the trees hung great lianas
like heads of hair or snakes.
There was a superstitious feeling in the air.
Below:
       the lemon-hued lagoon,
           like polished jade.
Cries would rise from the water
and the sound of mud-colored bodies plunging into water.
       A superstitious feeling . . .
The girls came and went, with their jars,
singing an old love-song as they passed.
Those who came up, erect as statues:
beneath their cool red amphorae with painted patterns,
       cool bodies, with the shape of amphorae.
And those who went down
       went prancing and dancing, leapt like deer,
their skirts unfolding in the wind like flowers.

[R. P.-M.]

35

EPIGRAMS

. . . but you will not escape from my iambs . . . —CATULLUS

1

I give you these verses, Claudia, because they belong to you.
I've written them plainly so you can understand them.
They're just for you, but if they bore you,
maybe one day they'll spread, all through Spanish America . . .
and if you also scorn the love that wrote them,
other women will dream of this love that was not meant for them.
And perhaps you'll see, Claudia, that these poems
(written to court you) inspire
in other loving couples who read them
the kisses that the poet did not inspire in you.

2

Be careful, Claudia, when you're with me,
because the slightest gesture, any word, a sigh
of Claudia, the slightest slip,
perhaps one day scholars will examine it,
and this dance of Claudia's will be remembered for centuries.
I've warned you, Claudia.

3

Of all these movies, Claudia, of these parties,
of these horse races,
nothing will be left for posterity
except the verses of Ernesto Cardenal to Claudia
      (if even that)
and Claudia's name that I put in those verses
and the names of my rivals, in case I decide to snatch them
from oblivion and to include them also in my verses
to make fun of them.

4

Others maybe'll earn a lot of money
but I've sacrificed that money
to write these songs to you

or to another girl I'll praise instead of you
or to nobody at all.

5

When I lost you we both lost:
I lost because you were what I loved most
and you lost because I was the one who loved you most.
But between the two of us you lose more than I do:
for I can love others the way I loved you
but you'll never be loved the way you were loved by me.

6

You girls who one day will read these verses all stirred up
and will dream about a poet:
know that I wrote them for a girl like you
and it was all in vain.

7

This will be my revenge:
that one day you'll hold in your hands the book of a famous poet
and you'll read these lines that the author wrote for you
and you won't even know it.

8

They told me you were in love with another man
and then I went off to my room
and I wrote that article against the Government
that landed me in jail.

9

She was sold to Kelly & Martínez, Inc.,
and many people will send her silver wedding presents,
and others will send her silver-plated presents,
and her one-time lover sends her this epigram.

10

You who are proud of my verses

not because I wrote them
but because you inspired them
even though they were written against you:

> You might have inspired better poetry.
> You might have inspired better poetry.

11

I've handed out underground leaflets,
shouting Long Live Freedom! in the middle of the street
defying the armed guards.
I took part in the April Rebellion:
but I grow pale when I pass by your house
and one glance from you makes me tremble.

12

Take these Costa Rican roses,
Myriam, with these love verses:
my verses will remind you that rose faces
are like your face; the roses
will remind you that love must be cut off
and that your face will fade like Greece and Rome.
When there is no more love or Costa Rican roses,
you'll remember, Myriam, this sad song.

13   *Imitation of Propertius*
I sing not of the defense of Stalingrad
or of the Egyptian Campaign
or of the landing on Sicily
or of General Eisenhower's crossing of the Rhine:

I sing only of the courting of a girl.

Not with the jewels of the Morlock Jewelry Store
nor with Dreyfus Perfumes
nor with orchids inside their plastic box
nor with a Cadillac

but just with my poems I courted her.

And she prefers me, even though I'm poor, to all Somoza's millions.

14

You've worked twenty years
to pile up twenty million *pesos,*
but we'd give twenty million *pesos*
not to have to work the way you've worked.

15

You don't deserve even an epigram.

16

I still remember that street with yellow lamps,
with that full moon between the electric wires,
and that star on the corner, a far-off radio,
the Merced Church tower striking eleven:
and the golden light of your open door, on that street.

17

Our love was born in May with *malinches* in flower—
when the *malinches* are in flower in Managua—.
They flower only in that month: in other months they bear vexations.
But the *malinches* will flower again in May
and the love that's gone won't return again.

18

Suddenly in the night the sirens
sound their long, long, long alarm,
the siren's miserable howl
of fire, or death's white ambulance
like a ghost wailing in the night,
coming closer and closer above the streets
and the houses, it rises, rises, and falls,
and it grows, grows, falls and goes away
growing and dying. It's neither a fire nor a death:

Just the Dictator flashing by.

19

Some shots were heard last night.
Out by the burial ground.
No one knows who they killed, or how many.
No one knows a thing.
Some shots were heard last night.
That's all.

20

You are alone among the crowds
as the moon is alone
and the sun is alone in the sky.

Yesterday you were in the stadium
in the midst of thousands of people
and I spotted you as soon as I entered
just as if you'd been alone
in an empty stadium.

21

If you are in New York
in New York there's nobody else
and if you're not in New York
in New York there's nobody.

22

But in the night you see your rice and your fried beans,
with a fresh cheese and a hot tortilla,
or a roast banana,
            you eat them without a bodyguard.
And your pitcher of cocoa is not first tasted by an adjutant.
And afterwards, if you want to, you can play a country song on
        your guitar,
and you don't sleep surrounded by floodlights and barbed wire
        and watchtowers.

23
Your eyes are a moon shimmering on a black lagoon
and your hair the black waves beneath the moonless sky
and the owl flying in the black night.

24
Yesterday I saw you on the street, Myriam, and
you looked so lovely to me, Myriam, that
(how can I explain to you how lovely you looked!)
not even you, Myriam, can see yourself so lovely or
imagine you can look so lovely to me.
And you looked so lovely that it seems to me that
no woman is lovelier than you
nor does any lover see any woman
so lovely, Myriam, as I see you
and even you, Myriam, can hardly be so lovely
(because so much loveliness can not be real!)
as the way I saw you yesterday so lovely on the street,
and as it seems to me today, Myriam, that I saw you.

25
Recall the many lovely girls that have existed:
all the beauties of Troy, and those of Achæa
and those of Thebes, and of the Rome of Propertius.
And many of them let love pass by,
and they died, and they've been dead for centuries.
You who are lovely now on the streets of Managua,
like them one day you'll belong to a distant past,
when the gas stations will be romantic ruins.

Remember the beauties of the streets of Troy!

26
Ah, you, pitiless one,
              crueler than young Tacho.

27

There is a place next to the Tiscapa Lagoon—
a bench under a *quelite* tree—
that you know (the girl I'm writing
these verses for will know they're for her).
And you remember that bench and that *quelite*;
the moon reflected in the Tiscapa Lagoon,
the lights of the dictator's palace,
the frogs croaking down there in the lagoon.
That *quelite* tree is still there;
the same lights still shine;
the moon is reflected in the Tiscapa Lagoon;
but tonight that bench will be empty,
or it will have another couple, not us.

28

My sweet kitten, my sweet kitten!
How my sweet kitten trembles
as I stroke her face and neck
and as you murder and torture!

29

In Costa Rica the teamsters sing.
They travel the roads with mandolins.
And the carts go by painted like parrots,
and the oxen move with colored ribbons
and little bells and flowers on their horns.

When it's coffee picking time in Costa Rica
and the carts go by loaded with coffee.

And there are bands in the town squares,
and in San José the balconies and windows
are filled with girls and flowers.
And the girls stroll around the park.
And the President can walk the streets in San José.

30   *Epitaph for the Tomb of Adolfo Báez Bone*
They killed you and they wouldn't tell us where they buried your body,
but ever since the whole country has been your tomb;
or rather: in every inch of the country where your body does not lie,
you have risen from the dead.

They thought they were killing you with an order to fire.
They thought they were burying you
and what they were doing was burying a seed.

31   *Somoza Unveils Somoza's Statue of Somoza in the Somoza Stadium*
It's not that I think the people raised this statue to me,
because I know better than you do that I ordered it myself.
Nor that I have any illusions about passing with it into posterity
because I know the people one day will tear it down.
Nor that I wished to erect to myself in life
the monument you'll not erect to me in death:
I put up this statue just because I know you'll hate it.

32
Every evening she'd walk with her mother along the Landestrasse
and at the corner of the Schmiedtor, every evening,
there was Hitler waiting for her, to watch her go by.
The taxis and the buses were filled with kisses
and the couples rented boats on the Danube.
But he didn't know how to dance. He never dared to speak to her.
Later she'd go by without her mother, with a cadet.
And still later she didn't go by at all.
That's why we had the Gestapo, the annexation of Austria,
the World War.

33   *Epitaph for Joaquín Pasos*
Here he walked, through these streets, unemployed, jobless,
and without a nickel.
Only poets, whores, and drunkards knew his verses.
He never went abroad.
He was in prison.

Now he's dead.
He has no monument.
                    But
remember him when you have concrete bridges,
great turbines, tractors, silver-colored granaries,
good governments.
Because in his poems he purified his people's language
which one day will be used to write the commercial treaties,
the Constitution, the love letters, and the decrees.

34
The National Guard is out searching for a man.
A man is hoping tonight to reach the frontier.
The name of that man is not known.
There are many more men buried in a trench.
The numbers and the names of those men are not known.
Nor are the location and the number of the trenches known.
The National Guard is out searching for a man.
A man is hoping tonight to escape from Nicaragua.

35
Our poems can't be published yet.
They circulate from hand to hand, in manuscript
or mimeograph. But one day
people will forget the name of the dictator
against whom they were written,
but they'll go on reading them.

36
Maybe we'll get married this year,
my love, and we'll have a little house.
And maybe my book'll get published,
or we'll both go abroad.
Maybe Somoza will fall, my love.

37   *A Girl's Song*
My long hair! My long hair!

You wanted your girl to have long hair.
Now I have it down below my shoulders
and you didn't wait for my long hair.

38
Do you think this corner with the woman selling guavas
where you met me with terror and with joy
(even if you showed only pallor and silence)
will be wiped out by Los Angeles and the Champs-Élysées?

39   *Corn-Island*
The water of South West Bay is bluer than the sky
but your eyes are bluer than South West Bay
and in Brig Bay Cave there is a pirate treasure
but your curls are worth more than the treasure of Brig Bay.

40
Now the May rains have come,
the scarlet *malinches* have blossomed again
and Diriá Road is joyful, full of puddles:
                    but now you are not with me.

41
Haven't you read, my love, in the *News*:
SENTINEL OF PEACE, GENIUS OF WORK
PALADIN OF DEMOCRACY IN AMERICA
DEFENDER OF CATHOLICISM IN AMERICA
THE PROTECTOR OF THE PEOPLE
                    THE BENEFACTOR . . . ?
They plunder the people's language.
And they falsify the people's words.
(Just like the people's money.)
That's why we poets do so much polishing on a poem.
And that's why my love poems are important.

42
We wake up with guns going off

and the dawn alive with planes—
It sounds like a revolution:
it's only the Tyrant's birthday.

43
Ileana: the Galaxy of Andromeda,
at 700,000 light years,
that the naked eye can see on a clear night,
is closer than you.
Other solitary eyes will be looking at me from Andromeda,
in their night. You I do not see.
Ileana: distance is time, and time flies.
At 200 million miles an hour the universe
is expanding toward nothingness.
And you are like millions of years away from me.

44
As the jackiedaw sings at night
to the jackdaw on another branch:
   Jackdaw,
  if you want me to go, I'll go
  if you want me to go, I'll go
and the jackdaw calls her to his branch:
   Jackiedaw,
  if you want to come, come
  if you want to come, come
and when she goes off to where he is
the jackdaw goes off to another branch:
  so I call to you
    and you go off.
  So I call to you
    and off you go.

45
If at the time of the April revolt
I'd been killed with the rest
I wouldn't have known you:

and if the April revolt had come now
I'd have been killed with the rest.

46
When the golden asters blossomed
we were both in love.
The asters still have blossoms
and now we're a couple of strangers.

47
The heavy drops are like
footsteps climbing the stairs
and the wind beating against the door
like a woman about to come in.

48
You came to visit me in dreams
but the emptiness you left behind when you went away
was real.

49
The person closest to me
is you, and yet
I haven't seen you for ages
except in dreams.

50
Have you heard in the night the cry of the anteater
      oo-oo-oo-oo
or the coyote in the moonlit night
      uuuuuuuuuuuuuuuuuuu?
Well, that's just what these verses are.

[1–17, 20–41, 43–50 D. D. W.; 18–19, 42 T. M.]

Tropical nights in Central America,
with moonlit lagoons and volcanoes
and lights from presidential palaces,
barracks and sad curfew warnings.
"Often while smoking a cigarette
I've decided that a man should die,"
says Ubico smoking a cigarette . . .
In his pink-wedding-cake palace
Ubico has a head cold. Outside, the people
were dispersed with phosphorous bombs.
San Salvador laden with night and espionage,
with whispers in homes and boardinghouses
and screams in police stations.
Carías' palace stoned by the people.
A window of his office has been smashed,
and the police have fired upon the people.
And Managua the target of machine guns
from the chocolate-cookie palace
and steel helmets patrolling the streets.

Watchman! What hour is it of the night?
Watchman! What hour is it of the night?

The *campesinos* of Honduras used to carry their money in their hats
when the *campesinos* sowed their seed
and the Hondurans were masters of their land.
When there was money
and there were no foreign loans
or taxes for J. P. Morgan & Co.,
and the fruit company wasn't competing with the little dirt farmer.
But the United Fruit Company arrived
with its subsidiaries the Tela Railroad Company
and the Trujillo Railroad Company
allied with the Cuyamel Fruit Company
and Vaccaro Brothers & Company
later Standard Fruit & Steamship Company
of the Standard Fruit & Steamship Corporation:

                    the United Fruit Company
with its revolutions for the acquisition of concessions
and exemptions of millions in import duties
and export duties, revisions of old concessions
and grants for new exploitations,
violations of contracts, violations
of the Constitution . . .
And all the conditions are dictated by the Company
with liabilities in case of confiscation
(liabilities of the nation, not of the Company)
and the conditions imposed by the latter (the Company)
for the return of the plantations to the nation
(given free by the nation to the Company)
at the end of 99 years . . .
"and all the other plantations belonging
to any other person or companies or enterprises
which may be dependents of the contractors and in which
this latter has or may have in the future
any interest of any kind will be as a consequence
included in the previous terms and conditions . . ."
(Because the Company also corrupted prose.)
The condition was that the Company build the Railroad,
but the Company wasn't building it,
because in Honduras mules were cheaper than the Railroad,
and "a Gongressman was chipper than a mule,"
                    as Zemurray used to say,
even though he continued to enjoy tax exemptions
and a grant of 175,000 acres for the Company,
with the obligation to pay the nation for each mile
that he didn't build, but he didn't pay anything to the nation
even though he didn't build a single mile (Carías is the dictator
who didn't build the greatest number of miles of railroad)
and after all, that shitty railroad was
of no use at all to the nation
because it was a railroad between two plantations
and not between the cities of Trujillo and Tegucigalpa.

They corrupt the prose and they corrupt the Congress.
The banana is left to rot on the plantations,
or to rot in the cars along the railroad tracks
or it's cut overripe so it can be rejected
when it reaches the wharf or be thrown into the sea;
the bunches of bananas declared bruised, or too skinny,
or withered, or green, or overripe, or diseased:
so there'll be no cheap bananas,
        or so as to buy bananas cheap.
Until there's hunger along the Atlantic Coast of Nicaragua.

And the farmers are put in jail for not selling at 30 cents
and their bananas are slashed with bayonets
and the Mexican Trader Steamship sinks their barges on them
and the strikers are cowed with bullets.
(And the Nicaraguan congressmen are invited to a garden party.)
But the black worker has seven children.
And what can you do? You've got to eat.
And you've got to accept what they offer to pay.
        24 cents a bunch.
While the Tropical Radio Subsidiary was cabling Boston:
"We assume that Boston will give its approval to
the payment made to the Nicaraguan congressmen of the majority party
because of the incalculable benefits that it represents for the Company."
And from Boston to Galveston by telegraph
and from Galveston by cable and telegraph to Mexico
and from Mexico by cable to San Juan del Sur
and from San Juan del Sur by telegraph to Puerto Limón
and from Puerto Limón by canoe way into the mountains
arrives the order of the United Fruit Company:
"United is buying no more bananas."
And workers are laid off in Puerto Limón.
And the little workshops close.
Nobody can pay his debts.
And the bananas rotting in the railroad cars.
        So there'll be no cheap bananas
        And so that there'll be bananas cheap,

19 cents a bunch.
The workers get IOUs instead of wages.
Instead of payment, debts.
And the plantations are abandoned, for they're useless now,
and given to colonies of unemployed.
And the United Fruit Company in Costa Rica
with its subsidiaries the Costa Rica Banana Company
and the Northern Railway Company and
the International Radio Telegraph Company
and the Costa Rica Supply Company
               are fighting in court against an orphan.
The cost of a derailment is $25 in damages
(but it would have cost more to repair the track).

And congressmen, cheaper than mules, Zemurray used to say.
Sam Zemurray, the Turkish banana peddler
in Mobile, Alabama, who one day took a trip to New Orleans
and on the wharves saw United throwing bananas into the sea
and he offered to buy all the fruit to make vinegar,
he bought it, and he sold it right there in New Orleans
and United had to give him land in Honduras
to get him to break his contract in New Orleans,
and that's how Sam Zemurray abbointed bresidents in Jonduras.
He provoked border disputes between Guatemala and Honduras
(which meant between the United Fruit Company and *his* company)
proclaiming that Honduras (*his* company) must not lose
"one inch of land not only in the disputed strip
but also in any other zone of Honduras
(of his company) not in dispute . . ."
(while United was defending the rights of Honduras
in its lawsuit with Nicaragua Lumber Company)
until the suit ended because he merged with United
and afterward he sold all his shares to United
and with the proceeds of the sale he bought shares in United
and with the shares he captured the presidency of Boston
(together with its employees the various presidents of Honduras)
and he was now the owner of both Honduras and Guatemala

and that was the end of the lawsuit over the exhausted lands
that were now of no use either to Guatemala or Honduras.

There was a Nicaraguan abroad,
a "Nica" from Niquinohomo,
working for the Huasteca Petroleum Co. of Tampico.
And he had five thousand dollars saved up.
And he wasn't a soldier or a politician.
And he took three thousand of the five thousand dollars
and went off to Nicaragua to join Moncada's revolution.
But by the time he arrived, Moncada was laying down his arms.
He spent three days miserable in the Peoples Hill.
Miserable, not knowing what to do.
And he wasn't a politician or a soldier.
He thought and thought and he finally said to himself:
"Somebody's got to do it."
                    And then he issued his first proclamation.

General Moncada sends a wire to the Americans:
ALL MY MEN AGREE TO SURRENDER EXCEPT ONE.
Mr. Stimson sends him an ultimatum,
"The people thanks you for nothing . . ."
                        is Moncada's message to the hold-out.
He assembles his men in El Chipote:
29 men (and with him, 30) against the U.S.A.
        EXCEPT ONE.
                    ("One from Niquinohomo . . .")
And with him, 30!
"Anyone who sets out to be a savior winds up on the Cross,"
says Moncada in another message.
Because Moncada and Sandino were neighbors;
Moncada from Masatepe and Sandino from Niquinohomo.
And Sandino replies to Moncada:
"Death is quite unimportant."
And to Stimson: "I have faith in the courage of my men . . ."
And to Stimson, after the first defeat:
"Anybody that thinks we're defeated

doesn't know my men."
And he wasn't a soldier or a politician.
And his men:
             many of them were kids,
with palm-leaf hats and sandals
or barefoot, with machetes, old men
with white beards, twelve-year-olds with their rifles,
whites, inscrutable Indians, and blonds, and kinky-haired blacks
with tattered pants and with no provisions,
their pants in shreds,
parading in Indian file with the flag up front—
a rag hoisted on a branch from the woods—
silent beneath the rain, and weary,
their sandals sloshing in the puddles of the town
                    Long live Sandino!
and they came down from the mountain and they went back up to
      the mountain,
marching, sloshing, with the flag up front.
A barefoot or sandaled army with almost no weapons
that had neither discipline nor disorder
where neither officers nor troops got any pay
but nobody was forced to fight:
and they had different military ranks but they were all equal,
everybody getting the same food
and clothing, the same ration for everybody.
And the officers had no aides:
more like a community than an army
and more united by love than by military discipline
even though there has never been greater unity in an army.
A happy army, with guitars and hugs.
A love song was its battle hymn:

          "If Adelita went off with another guy
          I'd go after her by land and by sea.
          If by sea on an armored cruiser
          And if by land on an armored train."

"We all greet each other with hugs,"
Sandino used to say—and nobody hugged like him.
And whenever they talked about themselves they'd say "all":
"All of us . . ." "We're all equal."
"Here we're all brothers," Umanzor used to say.
And they were all united until they were all killed.
Fighting against airplanes with hayseed troops,
with no pay except food and clothing and arms,
and hoarding each bullet as though it were made of gold;
with mortars made out of pipes
and with bombs made out of rocks and pieces of glass,
stuffed with dynamite from the mines and wrapped in hides;
with hand grenades made of sardine cans.

"He's a *bandido*," Somoza used to say, "a *bandolero*."
And Sandino never owned any property.
Which, translated, means:
it was Somoza calling Sandino an outlaw.
And Sandino never owned any property.
And at banquets Moncada called him a bandit
and up in the mountains Sandino had no salt
and his men shivering with cold in the mountains,
and he mortgaged his father-in-law's house
in order to free Nicaragua, while in the Presidential Mansion
Moncada had Nicaragua mortgaged.
"Of course he isn't one," said the American Minister
laughing, "but we call him a bandit technically."

What's that light way off there? Is it a star?
It's Sandino's light shining in the black mountain.
There they are, he and his men, beside the red bonfire
with rifles slung and wrapped in their blankets,
smoking or singing sad songs from the North,
the men motionless and their shadows in motion.

His face was as vague as that of a ghost,
remote because of his brooding and thinking

and serious because of the campaigns and the wind and the rain.
And Sandino had the face not of a soldier
but of a poet changed into a soldier through necessity,
and of a nervous man controlled by serenity.
There were two faces superposed on his face:
a countenance somber and yet radiant;
sad as a mountain evening
and joyful as a mountain morning.
In the light his face became young again,
and in the shadow it filled with weariness.
And Sandino wasn't intelligent or cultured.
But he turned out to have mountain intelligence.
"In the mountain everything is a teacher," Sandino used to say
(dreaming of Segovias filled with schools)
and he got messages from all the mountains
and it seemed as if every cabin was spying for him
(where foreigners were like brothers,
all foreigners, even the Americans)
            "even the Yankees . . ."
And: "God will speak through the Segovians . . ." he would say.
"I never thought I'd come out of this war alive
but I've always believed it was a necessary war . . ."
And: "Do they think I'm going to turn into a big landowner?"

It's midnight in the Segovia Mountains.
And that light is Sandino! A light with a song . . .

            "If Adelita went off with another guy."

But nations have their destiny.
And Sandino never became president.
It was Sandino's murderer who became president
and he was president for 20 years!

            "If Adelita went off with another guy
            I'd go after her by land and by sea."

The truce was signed. They loaded the arms onto wagons.
Blunderbusses held together with hemp rope, scaly rifles
and a few old machine guns.
And the wagons came down through the mountains.

> "If by sea on an armored cruiser
> And if by land on an armored train."

A telegram from the American Minister (Mr. Lane)
to the Secretary of State, sent in Managua
on the 14th of February 1934 at 6:05 p.m.
and received in Washington at 8:50 p.m.
> "Informed by official sources
> that the plane could not land in Wiwilí
> and that Sandino's arrival is therefore delayed . . ."

The telegram of the American Minister (Mr. Lane)
to the Secretary of State on the 16th of February
announcing Sandino's arrival in Managua
Not Printed
was not printed in the State Dept. memorandum.

Like the paca that came out of the thicket
onto the highway and is surrounded by dogs
and stands still facing the hunters
because it knows it has nowhere to go . . .

"I talked with Sandino for half an hour,"
said Somoza to the American Minister,
"but I can't tell you what he talked about
because I don't know what he talked about,
because I don't know what he talked about."

"And so, you see, I'll never own any property" . . .
And "It is un-con-sti-tu-tion-al," Sandino would say.
"The National Guard is unconstitutional."
"An insult!" said Somoza to the American Minister

on the TWENTY-FIRST OF FEBRUARY at 6:00 p.m.
"An insult! I want to stop Sandino."

Four prisoners are digging a hole.
"Who's dead?" asked one prisoner.
"Nobody," said the guard.
"Then what's the hole for?"
"None of your business," said the guard, "Go on digging."

The American Minister is having lunch with Moncada.
"Will you have coffee, sir?"
Moncada sits looking out the window.
"Will you have coffee, sir?
 It's very good coffee, sir."
"What?" Moncada looks away from the window
toward the servant: "Oh, yes, I'll have coffee."
And he laughed, "Certainly."

In a barracks five men are in a locked room
with guards at the doors and windows.
One of the men has only one arm.
The fat bemedaled officer comes in and he says to them: "Yes."

Another man is going to have supper with the President that night
(the man for whom they were digging the hole)
and he tells his friends: "Let's go. It's time."
And they go up to have supper with the President of Nicaragua.

At 10:00 p.m. they drive down to Managua.
Halfway down the guards stop them.
The two oldest are taken off in one car
and the other three in another car in another direction,
to where four prisoners had been digging a hole.
"Where are we going?"
asked the man they made the hole for.
                    And nobody answered him.

Then the car stopped and a guard said to them:
"Get out." The three of them got out,
and a one-armed man shouted: "Fire!"

"I was at a concert," said Somoza.
And it was true, he had been at a concert
or at a banquet or watching a dancer dance or
at some crap or other.
And at 10 o'clock that night Somoza was scared.
Suddenly out there the phone rang.
"Sandino is on the phone!"
And he was scared. One of his friends said:
"Don't be an idiot, you goddamned fool!"
Somoza said not to answer the phone.
The dancer went on dancing for the murderer.
And out there in the dark the phone went on
                    ringing and ringing.

By the light of a flood lamp
four guards are filling in a hole.
And by the light of a February moon.

It's the hour when the corn-mush star of Chontales
gets the little Indian girls up to make corn mush,
and out come the chicle-seller, the wood-seller, and the root-seller,
with the banana groves still silvered by the moon,
with the cry of the coyote and the honey bear
and the hooting of the owl in the moonlight.
The pacas and the agoutis come out of their holes
and the tickbirds and the *cadejos* hide in theirs.
The Weeper goes weeping along the river banks:
"D'you find him?" "No!" "D'you find him?" "No!"
A bird cackles like the creaking of a tree,
then the ravine is hushed as if listening to something,
and suddenly a scream . . . The bird utters
the same sad word, the same sad word.
The ranch hands begin to herd their cows:

Tooo-to-to-to; Tooo-to-to-to; Tooo-to-to-to;
the boatmen hoist the sails of their boats;
the telegraph clerk in San Rafael del Norte wires:
GOOD MORNING ALL IS WELL IN SAN RAFAEL DEL NORTE
and the telegraph clerk in Juigalpa: ALL IS WELL IN JUIGALPA.
And the Tuca squaws keep coming down the Hidden River
with the ducks going quack-quack-quack, and the echoes,
the echoes, while the tugboat goes with the Tuca squaws
slithering over the green-glass river
toward the Atlantic . . .

And meanwhile in the drawing rooms of the Presidential Mansion
and in the prison yards and in the barracks
and in the American Legation and in the Police Station
those who kept watch that night saw one another in the ghostly dawn
with hands and faces as though stained with blood.

"I did it," Somoza said afterward.
"I did it, for the good of Nicaragua."

And William Walker said, when they were going to execute him:
"The President of Nicaragua is a Nicaraguan."

In April, in Nicaragua, the fields are dry.
It's the month of brush burning,
of heat, and pastures covered with embers,
and coal-colored hills;
of hot winds, and air that smells charred,
and of fields made blue by the smoke
and the dust clouds of the tractors uprooting trees;
of the riverbeds dry as roads
and the branches stripped like roots;
of suns blurred and blood-red
and moons huge and red as suns
and the far-off brush fires, at night, like stars.

In May come the first rains.

The tender grass is reborn from the ashes.
The muddy tractors plough the earth.
The roads fill with butterflies and puddles,
and the nights are cool, and insect-laden,
and it rains all night. In May
the *malinches* blossom in the streets of Managua.
But April in Nicaragua is the month of death.
They killed them in April.
I was with them in the April rebellion
and I learned to handle a Rising machine gun.
       And Adolfo Báez Bone was my friend:
They hunted him with airplanes, with trucks,
with floodlights, with tear-gas bombs,
with radios, with dogs, with police;
and I remember the red clouds over the Presidential Mansion
like blood-red swabs of cotton,
and the red moon over the Presidential Mansion.
The underground radio kept saying he was alive.
The people didn't believe he had died.
       (And he hasn't died.)

Because at times a man is born in a land
       and he *is* that land.
And the land in which that man is buried
       is that man.
And the men who afterward are born in that land
       are that man.
And Adolfo Báez Bone was that man.

"If they asked me to choose my fate"
(Báez Bone had said to me three days before)
"to choose between dying murdered like Sandino
or being President like Sandino's murderer
I'd choose Sandino's fate."
       And he did choose his fate.
Glory isn't what the history books teach:
it's a flock of buzzards in a field and a great stink.

But when a hero dies
      he doesn't die:
for that hero is reborn
      in a Nation.

Afterward the U.S.A. sent more arms to Somoza;
it took about half a morning for the arms to go by;
trucks and trucks loaded with crates of arms
all marked U.S.A. MADE IN U.S.A.,
arms to catch more prisoners, to hunt down books,
to steal five pesos from Juan Potosme.
I saw those arms going along Roosevelt Avenue.
And people silent in the streets watched them go by:
the skinny one, the barefoot one, the one with the bicycle,
the black one, the blubber-lipped, the girl dressed in yellow,
the tall one, the blond, the bald one, the one with the big mustache,
the snub-nosed one, the straight-haired, the kinky-haired, the squat one,
and the faces of all those people
      were the face of a dead ex-lieutenant.

The mambo music used to come down as far as Managua.
With his eyes red and blurred like the eyes of a shark
but a shark with a bodyguard and armaments
(*Nicaraguan shark*)
Somoza was dancing the mambo
           mambo mambo
           yummy mambo
when they were killing them.
And Tachito Somoza (the son) goes up to the Presidential Mansion
to change a blood-stained shirt
for a clean one.
      Stained with blood and chili.
The prison dogs would howl with pity.
People living near the barracks would hear the screams.
At first it was a single scream in the middle of the night,
and afterward more and more screams
and afterward a silence . . . Then a volley

and a single shot. Afterward another silence,
and an ambulance.

And in the jail the dogs are howling again!
The sound of the iron door closing
behind you and then the questions begin
and the accusation, the accusation of conspiracy
and the confession, and then the hallucinations,
the snapshot of your wife shining like a spotlight
in front of you and the nights filled with shrieks
and with noises and with silence, a tomblike silence,
and again the same question, the same question,
and the same noise repeated and the spotlight in your eyes
and then the long months that followed.
Oh, to be able to sleep in your own bed tonight
without the fear of being pulled out of bed and taken out of your house,
the fear of knocks on the door or doorbells ringing in the night!

Shots sound in the night, or they seem to be shots.
Heavy trucks go by, and they stop,
and they go on. You've heard their voices.
It's at the corner. They must be changing the guard.
You've heard their laughter and their weapons.
The tailor across the street has turned on his light.
And it seemed as though they knocked here. Or at the tailor's.
Maybe tonight you're on the list!
And the night goes on. And there's a lot of night left.
And the day will be only a sunlit night.
The quietness of night under the scorching sun.

Mr. Whelan, the American Minister,
attends the party at the Presidential Mansion.
The lights of the Mansion can be seen all over Managua.
The music from the party reaches even the prison cells
in the gentle breeze of Managua under Martial Law.
The prisoners in their cells manage to hear the music
among the screams of prisoners getting electric shocks.

Up at the Mansion Mr. Whelan says:
                    "Fine party!"

As the sonofabitch Roosevelt said to Sumner Welles:
"Somoza is a sonofabitch
                    but he's ours."

A slave to foreigners
                    and a tyrant to his people
imposed by intervention
                    and kept in power by nonintervention
SOMOZA FOREVER

The spy who goes out by day
The agent who goes out by night
and the night arrest:
Those who are jailed for talking on a bus
or for shouting Hurray
or for a joke.
"Accused of talking against His Excellency the President . . ."
And the ones judged by a toad-faced judge
or in Courts Martial with dog-faced guards;
and the ones forced to drink piss and eat shit
(when you all get a Constitution, remember them)
the ones with the bayonet in the mouth and the needle in the eye,
the electric shocks and the spotlight in the eyes.
"He's a sonofabitch, Mr. Welles, but he's *ours*."
And in Guatemala, in Costa Rica, in Mexico,
the exiles wake up at night screaming,
dreaming that they're getting the "little machine" again,
or that they're tied up once more
watching Tachito coming at them with the needle.
". . . And he was good-looking, you know . . .
                    (said a *campesino*).
"Yes, it was him. And good-looking, you know . . .
White skin, with his little yellow
short-sleeved shirt.

The good-looking bastard."

When night falls in Nicaragua the Presidential Mansion
fills with shadows. And faces appear.
Faces in the darkness.
                    Blood-covered faces.
Adolfo Báez Bone; Pablo Leal without a tongue;
my classmate Luis Gabuardi whom they burned alive
and he died shouting *Death to Somoza!*
The face of the sixteen-year-old telegraph clerk
(we don't even know his name)
who sent secret messages at night
to Costa Rica, trembling telegrams across
the night, from the dark Nicaragua of Tacho
(and the boy won't be mentioned in the history books)
and he was caught, and he died looking at Tachito;
his face is still looking at him. The kid
they caught at night sticking up posters
                SOMOZA IS A THIEF
and some laughing guards drag him off into the woods . . .
And so many other shadows, so many other shadows;
the shadows of the flocks of buzzards at Wilwilí;
the shadow of Estrada; the shadow of Umanzor;
the shadow of Socrates Sandino;
and the great shadow, the one of the great crime,
the shadow of Augusto César Sandino.
Every night in Managua the Presidential Mansion
fills with shadows.

But the hero is born when he dies
and green grass is reborn from the ashes.

[D. D. W.]

64

GETHSEMANI, KY.

1

Spring has come with its smell of Nicaragua:
smell of earth recently rained on, and smell of heat,
of flowers, of disinterred roots, wet leaves,
(and I have heard the lowing of distant cattle . . .)
—or is it the smell of love? But this love
is not yours. Love of country, is the Dictator's love
the fat Dictator with his sports clothes and panama hat:
He was the one who loved the country, stole it,
and possessed it. In that earth he lies embalmed:
while love has taken you away to a strange land.

2

Like the flights of ducks
that go over calling
that in the autumn nights go over calling
to lagoons in the south they never saw,
and do not know who takes them, nor where they go,
so we are carried to Thee not knowing where.
Just like the flights of ducks that come from the south
and pass over Kentucky calling in the night.

3

There is a hum of tractors in the fields.
The cherry trees are pink with blossom.
And, look, the apple trees are in full bloom.
This, Beloved, is the season of love.
The starlings sing in the sycamore.
The roads smell of fresh tar
and passing cars bear laughing girls.
Look: the season of love has come.
Each bird that flies has one pursuing it.

4

Every evening the L&N
goes singing through these Kentucky fields
and I seem to hear the little train at home

in Nicaragua, when it borders the Managua Lake
across from the volcano, just before
Mateare, going around the bend
across from Bird Island, piping and singing
its iron song of wheels and rails,
with the first lights of Managua there
far off, shining in the waters . . .
The L&N goes off
into the distance with its song.

5

The sound of passing cars, (if a car comes)
on the highway outside the noviciate
is like sea surf. You hear one begin
to come far off and the sound grows
more and more, the motor roars,
tires sing on the damp tar
and then it goes away, dies down,
is no longer heard. Later some other engine
in the distance, begins to come again.
Like waves in the sea. And I, like waves
in the sea, once ran along tar roads that go
to no definite place. And still at times
it seems I go by the same roads
and do not stop going and arrive at no place,
that I am not the one in the noviciate
seeing the cars pass,
but that I have seen the noviciate
through the window of that car that just went by.

6

When the first signs go on
when they light up the marquees
of the movie theaters
here we hear nothing but swallows.
At 7 p.m. the Trappists go to bed
in broad daylight, like noon,

and with a full moon like midnight.
The horses are quiet in the stable.
The trucks sleep in the garage.
The tractors are still
before the barn.
Above the water tank: the aluminum moon.

7

The long freight train
wakes me in my cell
I hear it coming from far off
in the night. It passes and passes, whistling,
seeming that it will never all get past:
cars and cars and cars bumping along!
I fall asleep again, and it is still passing
panting in the distance and still whistling,
and between dreams I ask myself
why they still have trains
and where they take their freight, and what freight,
where the cars come from
and where they can possibly go.

8

The zinc roofs in the moonlight
and the tin shop, the gas tank
and the water tank, all look like silver.
Like a star, like a cigarette,
far out, over Nally's hill,
a passenger plane
passes and flashes in the night.

9

A dog barks far out
behind the black wood.
Further still
behind another wood,
another dog answers.

10

Like empty beer cans, like empty cigarette butts;
my days have been like that.
Like figures passing on a T.V. screen
and disappearing, so my life has gone.
Like cars going by fast on the roads
with girls laughing and radios playing . . .
Beauty got obsolete as fast as car models
and forgotten radio hits.
Nothing is left of those days, nothing,
but empty beer cans, cigarette butts,
smiles on faded photos, torn tickets
and the sawdust with which, in the mornings,
they swept out the bars.

11

A jet in the evening sky,
vapor like a thread,
as the sun sets, golden.
The plane too fast to see:
the golden flight lingers.

12

That auto horn sounds familiar.
So does this wind in the pines.
This zinc noviciate roof
reminds me of my house at home.
They are calling me with the auto horn.
But my house, near the road
where the cars went by all day
was sold years ago. Strangers live there.
This was no known car. It is gone.
The wind is the same. Only the sighing
of this rainy autumn evening is well known.

13

I turned out the light to see the snow,
and I saw snow through the window and a new moon.
But I saw that both snow and moon
were also a window pane
and that behind that pane you were watching me.

14

I do not know who is out in the snow.
All that is seen in the snow is his white habit
and at first I saw no one at all:
only the plain white sunlit snow.
A novice in the snow is barely visible.
And I feel that there is something more in this snow
which is neither snow nor novice, and is not seen.

15

The marmots in their burrows are not dead,
they sleep. Nor are the chipmunks dead,
nor have they gone away: curled up,
they lie asleep beneath the earth.
Adders sleep beneath dead leaves;
frogs, buried deep in frozen mud
down by the icebound river, also sleep.
The river sleeps as well. Life is asleep.
In caves, cracks, hollows, secret galleries,
eggs, silk cocoons, seeds, buds
all wait for spring. There are tracks in the snow:
the tracks of fox and skunk, each going out
by night, already searching for a mate.
There is a smell of skunk, these nights.

16

Behind the monastery, down by the road,
there is a cemetery of worn-out things
where lie smashed china, rusty metal,
cracked pipes and twisted bits of wire,

empty cigarette packs, sawdust,
corrugated iron, old plastic, tires beyond repair:
all waiting for the Resurrection, like ourselves.

[1–2, 4–10, 12–14 T. M.; 3, 11, 15–16 R. P.-M.]

THE VALE OF CUERNAVACA FROM THE MONASTERY

When there's been rain,
the air above the Vale is even clearer:
            the smoke of huts yet whiter
                        the volcanoes a deeper blue
            the bells yet more distinct.

                A barefoot lad
                drives cattle
                down the stony track.

On the blue mountains, even bluer shadows:
            shadows of contours
or perhaps of clouds.
                (And a single small red bird
                        on the telephone wire.)

The smoke of the huts rises
among the corn: and that of the brick kiln.
There is a factory a long way off, at the very
foot of the hills, whose smoke is far far higher.
                        And on the bluish plateau
the long smoke of a train, and its long whistle.

The sound of cars accelerating,
and buses, down on the main road.
                And the tap tap of the stonebreaker
                hammering away at his stones.
On this side: a heavy truck
                grinding up a hill. . . .

Goats pass with tinkling bells,
leave lingering on the air
a gentle smell of goat
and goat's milk.
                The birds are singing;
in Santa María de Ahuacatitlán
bells are ringing.

The setting sun gilds Teposteco
and tinges the snow on Popo pink.
          Cone
like strawberry ice-cream.

The moon comes up behind
Popocatépetl.

          .   .   .

(A moon tenuous as a cloud
and a cloud above Popo like snow
with Popo's snow the moon.)

          .   .   .

The lights of Cuernavaca twinkle in the distance:
those of Cuautla too, farther, almost in the sky,
tiny and bunched together, almost among the stars.
Somewhere in the fields a radio, playing a *corrido*.
A million crickets chirping in the pastures.
          Each chirps and stops and chirps.
Do crickets never sleep?
                    And fireflies
flicker like stars, like Cuautla,
like Cuernavaca.

          .   .   .

A train whistles in the distance,
deep in the night.
          Mournfully,
three times.
The old train to the capital,
like a lonely bird
calling its missing mate.

                                        [R. P.-M.]

ON LAKE NICARAGUA

Slow cargo-launch, midnight, mid-lake,
bound from San Miguelito to Granada.
The lights ahead not yet in sight,
the dwindling ones behind completely gone.
Only the stars
(the mast a finger pointing to the Seven Sisters)
            and the moon, rising above Chontales.

Another launch (just one red light) goes by
and sinks into the night.
We, for them:
            another red light sinking in the night . . .

And I, watching the stars, lying on the deck
between bunches of bananas and Chontales cheeses,
wonder: perhaps there's one that is an earth like ours
and someone's watching me (watching the stars)
from another launch, on another night, on another lake.

[R. P.-M.]

APOCALYPSE, 1960–1969

MANAGUA 6:30 P.M.

In the evening the neon lights are soft
and the mercury streetlamps, pale and beautiful . . .
And the red star on a radio tower
in the twilight sky of Managua
looks as pretty as Venus
and an ESSO sign looks like the moon

The red taillights of the cars are mystical

(The soul is like a girl kissed hard behind a car)
      TACA BUNGE KLM SINGER
      MENNEN HTM GÓMEZ NORGE
      RPM SAF ÓPTICA SELECTA
all proclaim the glory of God!
(Kiss me under the glowing signs oh God)
      KODAK TROPICAL RADIO F&C REYES
they spell your Name
in many colors.
          "They broadcast
the news . . ."
I don't know
what else they mean
I don't defend the cruelty behind these lights
And if I have to give a testimony about my times
it's this: They were primitive and barbaric
but poetic

[J. C.]

When fox cubs are born and tadpoles hatch
and the male butterfly dances in front of the female
and the kingfishers touch beaks
and the light grows longer and ovaries swell,
the swallows will return from the South. . . .
Will "return" from the South?
                              "The dark swallows"
those that flew off in September to North Africa,
crowded every curving loop of wire,
darkened the afternoons,
and filled the sky with voices,
those will not return.

And the eels that swam downriver in Africa
and sought the Sargasso Sea to consummate
their nuptials clad in silver wedding garments,
like the ladies of the Court of King Don Juan:
where are they now?
                      The *palolos* of the Southern Seas
which rise to the surface at their feast of fecundation
when the November moon is at its full
and cover the whole sea those nights with phosphorescent foam
and sink back beneath the sea not to return?

And the gilded *catopsilias* garbed like Queen Thi
that migrate each autumn NNW
leaving behind the nectar, flowers, the mating
with nothing ahead save billows, salt, sea-loneliness
and death (lying NNW)
            North-North-West
but on a steady bearing NNW?

[R. P.-M.]

GIVE EAR TO MY WORDS (PSALM 5)

Give ear to my words O Lord
                              Hear my groans
Listen to my protest
For you are not a God who is a friend of dictators
nor a supporter of their politics
nor are you influenced by their propaganda
nor do you associate with any gangster

There's no honesty in their speeches
nor in their press releases

They talk of peace in their speeches
while they increase their war production

They talk of peace at Peace Conferences
and secretly prepare for war

                 Their lying radios blare all night long

Their desks are piled with criminal plans
                              and sinister documents

But you will protect me from their plans

They speak through the mouth of machine guns
Their flashing tongues
                      are bayonets . . .

Punish them O God
             foil their politics
mix up their memos
                      block their programs

At the hour of the Alarm Siren
you will be with me
you will be my refuge on the day of the Bomb

You bless the righteous
who don't believe in the lies of their ads
nor in their publicity and political campaigns

Your love surrounds them
　　　　　　　like armored tanks

[J. C.]

Lords defenders of Law and Order:
Your justice is it not perhaps class justice?
        Civil Courts to protect private property
        Criminal Courts to dominate the dominated
The freedom you talk about is freedom for capital
    your "free world" means freedom to exploit
Your law is the shotgun and your order the jungle
    you own the police
    you own the judges
There are no landowners or bankers in your jails.

The bourgeois begins to go astray at his mother's breast
he has class prejudices from the day he's born
    like the rattlesnake he's born with his poison sac
    like the tiger shark he's born a man-eater

O God put an end to the status quo
        tear out the fangs of the oligarchs
Let them be flushed away like the water in the basin
    let them wither like weeds beneath the weed-killer

They are the "worms" when the Revolution comes
They are not body cells but microbes
    Miscarriages of the new man, they must be cast out
Before they bear thorns let the tractor uproot them

The common man will take his ease in the exclusive clubs
he will take over private enterprises
the just man will rejoice in the People's Courts
We shall celebrate in spacious squares the anniversary of the Revolution
    The God that exists is the God of the common man

[D. D. W.]

THE COSMOS IS HIS SANCTUARY (PSALM 150)

Praise the Lord in the cosmos
                              His sanctuary
with a radius of a hundred thousand million light years
Praise Him through the stars
                              and the interstellar spaces
Praise Him through the galaxies
                                   and the intergalactic spaces
Praise Him through the atoms
                              and the interatomic voids
Praise Him with the violin and the flute
                                   and with the saxophone
Praise Him with the clarinets and with the horn
     with bugles and trombones
                                   with cornets and trumpets
Praise Him with violas and cellos
                              with pianos and pianolas
Praise Him with blues and jazz
                              and with symphonic orchestras
with spirituals
          and with Beethoven's Fifth
     with guitars and marimbas
Praise Him with record players
                         and with magnetic tapes
Let everything that breathes praise the Lord
     every living cell
               Hallelujah

[D. D. W.]

82

Paradise is not on Paria
                    as Christopher Columbus thought
. . . most pretty countryside, as green and beauteous
as the orchards of Valencia in March . . .
. . . mildest temperateness, the countryside and trees
like April in the orchards of Valencia . . .
Nor
on Antigua where the temperature doesn't go higher than 80
and the bathing is just perfect, and there is electricity
and no malaria, and there are three golf courses
nor on Grenada, free of tropical diseases and hurricanes
with tennis courts, golf and a night-club
nor
on Saint Lucia
                    paradise of painters and photographers
nor on Cayman Island (free of income tax)
where you can still hunt for pirate treasure
and live in a hotel for $6 a day.
No. It doesn't come through the Tourist Agencies.
You have been saying ever since Calvary:
                    "today you shall be with me in Paradise . . ."
And it isn't Tobago
                    only 7 hours from New York
         A MODERATELY PRICED TROPICAL PARADISE
where a couple can live on $2000 a year
in a bungalow next to the sea, with electricity and radio
among guavas coco-palms mangos exotic flowers
and rum is cheap, and you don't spend money on clothes
because you can always wear shorts and sport shirts
Nor the Virgin Islands (British)
                    "a perfect paradise
except for the inconvenience of being without a dentist"
But I know Paradise
it isn't the one from the Tourist Agencies
                    Paradise is where the two of us are.

                                        [J. C.]

UNRIGHTEOUS MAMMON (LUKE 16:9)

In respect of riches, then, just or unjust,
of goods be they ill-gotten or well-gotten:
                         All riches are unjust.
All goods,
             ill-gotten.
If not by you, by others.
Your title deeds may be in order. But
did you buy your land from its true owner?
And he from its true owner? And the latter . . . ?
Though your title go back to the grant of a king
                         was
the land ever the king's?
Has no one ever been deprived of it?
And the money you receive legitimately now
from client or Bank or National Funds
             or from the U.S. Treasury,
was it ill-gotten at no point? Yet
do not think that in the Perfect Communist State
Christ's parables will have lost relevance
Or Luke 16:9 have lost validity
             and riches be no longer UNJUST
or that you will no longer have a duty to distribute riches!

[R. P.-M.]

84

PRAYER FOR MARILYN MONROE

Lord
receive this young woman known around the world as Marilyn Monroe
although that wasn't her real name
(but You know her real name, the name of the orphan raped at the age of 6
and the shopgirl who at 16 had tried to kill herself)
who now comes before You without any makeup
without her Press Agent
without photographers and without autograph hounds,
alone like an astronaut facing night in space.

She dreamed when she was little that she was naked in a church
                    (according to the *Time* account)
before a prostrated crowd of people, their heads on the floor
and she had to walk on tiptoe so as not to step on their heads.
You know our dreams better than the psychiatrists.
Church, home, cave, all represent the security of the womb
but something else too . . .
The heads are her fans, that's clear
(the mass of heads in the dark under the beam of light).
But the temple isn't the studios of 20th Century-Fox.
The temple—of marble and gold—is the temple of her body
in which the Son of Man stands whip in hand
driving out the studio bosses of 20th Century-Fox
who made Your house of prayer a den of thieves.

Lord
in this world polluted with sin and radioactivity
You won't blame it all on a shopgirl
who, like any other shopgirl, dreamed of being a star.
Her dream just became a reality (but like Technicolor's reality).
She only acted according to the script we gave her
—the story of our own lives. And it was an absurd script.
Forgive her, Lord, and forgive us
for our 20th Century
for this Colossal Super-Production on which we all have worked.
She hungered for love and we offered her tranquilizers.
For her despair, because we're not saints,

          psychoanalysis was recommended to her.
Remember, Lord, her growing fear of the camera
and her hatred of makeup—insisting on fresh makeup for each scene—
and how the terror kept building up in her
and making her late to the studios.

Like any other shopgirl
she dreamed of being a star.
And her life was unreal like a dream that a psychiatrist interprets and files.

Her romances were a kiss with closed eyes
and when she opened them
she realized she had been under floodlights
              as they killed the floodlights!
and they took down the two walls of the room (it was a movie set)
while the Director left with his scriptbook
               because the scene had been shot.
Or like a cruise on a yacht, a kiss in Singapore, a dance in Rio
the reception at the mansion of the Duke and Duchess of Windsor
      all viewed in a poor apartment's tiny living room.

The film ended without the final kiss.
She was found dead in her bed with her hand on the phone.
And the detectives never learned who she was going to call.
She was
like someone who had dialed the number of the only friendly voice
and only heard the voice of a recording that says: *WRONG NUMBER.*
Or like someone who had been wounded by gangsters
reaching for a disconnected phone.

Lord
whoever it might have been that she was going to call
and didn't call (and maybe it was no one
or Someone whose number isn't in the Los Angeles phonebook)
        You answer that telephone!

                                         [J. C.]

AND BEHOLD
    I saw an Angel
            (all his cells were electronic eyes)
and I heard a supersonic voice
saying: Open up thy typewriter and type
            and I beheld a silver projectile in flight
      which went from Europe to America in twenty minutes
and the name of the projectile was the H-Bomb
                        (and hell flew with it)
           and I saw a kind of flying saucer fall from heaven
And the seismographs plotted a shock like an earthquake
and all the artificial planets fell to earth
      and the President of the National Radiation Council
      the Director of the Atomic Energy Commission
      the Secretary of Defense
          were all deep in their sheltering caves
and the first Angel set off the warning siren
    and from the heavens rained Strontium 90
                Caesium 137
                Carbon 14
and the second Angel set off the warning siren
and all eardrums for 300 miles were shattered
by the sound of the explosion
all retinas which saw the flash of the explosion
were seared throughout those same 300 miles
         the heat at ground zero was like that of the sun
and steel and iron and glass and concrete were burnt up
         and sucked into the sides to fall as radioactive rain
and there was loosed a hurricane wind the force of Hurricane Flora
and three million cars and trucks flew up into the skies
and crashed into buildings bursting
                like Molotov cocktails
and the third Angel set off the warning siren
and I beheld a mushroom cloud above New York
             and a mushroom cloud above Moscow
    and a mushroom cloud above London
            and a mushroom cloud above Peking

(and Hiroshima's fate was envied)
And all the stores and all the museums and all the libraries
and all the beauties of the earth
                            were turned to vapor
and went to form part of the cloud of radioactive dust
which hung above the planet poisoning it
            the radioactive rain gave leukemia unto some
                              lung cancer unto others
          and unto others cancer of the bone
                          or cancer of the ovaries
children were born with cataracts
and the genes of man suffered unto the twenty-second generation.
                  And this was known as the 45-Minute War . . .
      Seven Angels came
bearing cups of smoke in their hands
                  (smoke like a mushroom cloud)
and first I saw the great cup raised over Hiroshima
                    (like a cone of venomous ice cream)
            engendering one vast malignant ulcer
and the cup of the second was poured into the sea
      making the whole sea radioactive
                          so that all the fishes died
and the third Angel poured forth a neutronic cup
and it was given unto him to sear men with a fire like solar fire
and the fourth Angel poured his cup which was of Cobalt
and it was given unto Babylon to drain the chalice of the grapes
                            of wrath
And the loud voice cried:
              Smite her with twice the megatons with which she smote!
And the Angel who controlled the firing of this bomb
                        pushed down the firing key
And they said unto me: Thou hast as yet not seen the Typhus Bomb
                  nor yet Q Fever
I continued watching the vision in the night
and in my vision I beheld as on TV
emerging from the masses
                  a Machine

                    fearful and terrible beyond all measure
and like a bear or an eagle or a lion with the wings of aircraft
many propellers numerous antennae eyes of radar
its brain a computer programmed to give the Number of the Beast
roaring through hosts of microphones
                              and it gave orders unto men
and all men went in fear of the Machine
Likewise I saw the aircraft in my vision
aircraft faster than sound bearing 50-megaton bombs
and no man guided them but the Machine alone
and they flew toward every city of the earth
each one precisely on target
And the Angel said: Canst thou see where Columbus Circle was?
              Or the place where the United Nations Building stood?
And where Columbus Circle was
                    I saw a hole which could contain a 50-story building
and where the United Nations Building stood
I saw only a great grey cliff covered with moss and duck shit
with wave-swept rocks beyond it and sea gulls crying
And in the heavens I beheld a mighty light
              like a million-megaton explosion
and I heard a voice saying unto me: Switch on thy radio
and I did switch it on and heard: BABYLON IS FALLEN
                         BABYLON THE GREAT IS
                                        FALLEN
and all transmitters in the world gave the same news
And the Angel gave me a check drawn on the National City Bank
and said unto me: Go thou cash this check
but no bank would for all the banks were bankrupt
Skyscrapers were as though they had never been
A million simultaneous fires yet not one firefighter
nor a phone to summon an ambulance nor were there any ambulances
nor was there enough plasma in all the world
                         to help the injured of a single city
And I heard another voice from heaven saying:
                         Go forth from her my people
Lest ye be contaminated by the Radiation

               lest ye be smitten by the Microbes
     by the Anthrax Bomb
          by the Cholera Bomb
      by the Diphtheria Bomb
             by the Tularemia Bomb
They will behold the great disaster on TV
              for the Bomb is fallen on great Babylon
and they will weep and wail for the Beloved City
pilots will look down from their planes afraid to approach
the ocean liners will stay anchored far away
for fear lest the atomic leprosy should fall on them
On every waveband there was a voice heard saying:
          ALLELUIA
And the Angel carried me away into the wilderness
       and the wilderness blossomed with laboratories
and there the Devil carried out his atomic tests
and I beheld the Great Whore riding on the Beast
(the Beast was a technological Beast all slogan-bedecked)
and the Whore came clutching all manner of checks and bonds
and shares and commercial documents
her harlot's voice sang drunkenly as in a night club
in her left hand she bore a cup of blood
and she was drunk with the blood of all those tortured
all those purged all those condemned by military courts
all those sent to the wall
and of whoever had resisted upon earth
               with all the martyrs of Jesus
and she laughed with her gold teeth
          the lipstick on her lips was blood
and the Angel said unto me: the heads which thou dost see on
    the Beast are dictators,
and their horns are revolutionary leaders who are not dictators yet
but they will be later
and these shall make war against the Lamb
           and the Lamb shall overcome them
And he said unto me: The nations of the world are split into 2 blocks
     (Gog and Magog)

yet the 2 blocks are in truth but the one
(which is against the Lamb)
                    and fire will fall from heaven to consume them both
And in the Earth's biology I saw a new Evolution
It was as though a New Planet had appeared in space
For death and hell were cast into the sea of nuclear fire
and neither were there peoples as before
but I saw rather a new species freshly evolved
a species not made up of individuals
but rather one sole organism
                                    made up of men in place of cells
and all biologists were mightily amazed
But men were free and in their union were one Person—
                                    not a Machine—
and the sociologists were equally astounded
Such men as had no part in this new species
                                    were but as fossils
The Organism enclosed the whole roundness of the planet
round as a cell (but planetary in dimensions)
and the Cell was garlanded as a Bride awaiting the Bridegroom
and the Earth rejoiced
        (as when, dividing, the first cell was wedded)
And there was a New Canticle
and all other inhabited planets heard the Earth singing
    and it was a love-song

[R. P.-M.]

Katún of dishonorable governors and many arrows,
of sadness in the huts,

                   and whispering,

     and vigilance by night.
In this *katún*
we weep for the books that were burned,
the exiles from the kingdom. The loss
of corn
and of our cosmic knowledge.

Greed and pestilence and rocks and skulls.

Lord Mountain Cat. Lord Honey Bear. The jaguar of the people.
In this *katún* the *chilán* writes:

              "the people eat stones

              eat sticks."
The *katún* in which great tributes are collected,

    in which the mask is stolen,
in which the treasure buried in the *milpa* is stolen.
In this *katún* invaders never lack;

              the enemies of the land.
Suckers of blood . . .

              Gnats battening on the peoples.
The emptiers of the great earthen jars.
Our life like badgers, in the jungle, is hard.
They scorn our knowledge of the universe:
a book in which we read for people's good.

    (In this *katún* we are derided for our dress.)

          The hieroglyphs are lost beneath the thickets.
Our Civilization with black vultures overhead.
Our dwellings flattened by the hurricane.
The Nobles now *peones* mending roads.
The people bowed down lugging a mountain in a net.
And governments: they are like the drought . . .
And we say: would that there might return

        he who first built an arch,

    wrote prayers,

devised the calendar permitting chronicles and histories
and auguries of things to come.
Now however, in the meanwhile, like badgers.
Saddest of moons,
saddest of moons in the sky of the Petén.
Oppression . . .
And vigilance in the night.
Our lord the Honey Bear is lecherous . . .

The *chilán* ("he that is mouth") writes thus:
"The Plague is great, and great the Hurricane"
In the blue sea the pointed fin
the pointed fin
of evil-minded Xooc, man-eating shark.

But the *katún* of the Cruel Men will pass.
The Katún of the Tree of Life shall be established.
And a benevolent rule.
The people be no longer bidden to eat less.
The Katún Union-for-a-Common-Cause,
the Katún of "Good living conditions."
No longer shall we have to keep our voices low.
The *chilán* says the people will be a united people.
Many will come together to sing together.
And then there will be no more Honey Bear.
The stone beneath the thickets will once more have a noble face.
The square stone
wear a countenance.

The governors will be good, to the people's joy.
The Lords: legitimate.
Abundance in the mountains, and fair rituals.

It is the time for building the new pyramid
upon the basis of the old.

The evil-minded Xooc, the Shark, has been harpooned.

And the people will never lack for a *chilán*.
The Chilán:

              he who reads the sacred scriptures
and studies the skies by night.
The movements of the Sun and of the Moon
in order that the time to till the land be known,
the time to harvest corn,

                    to burn the fields,
      to set the traps,
to search the woods for deer.
The Chilán: He sets the days for rain.
The days when men shall sing.
The ending of the rainy season.
Wards off both plagues and hunger.
Distributes food when hunger comes.
Invigilates the carving of the stelae,
     designs new temples,
delivers tablets which predict eclipses.

[R. P.-M.]

Things that now only Black Elk knew
and has wished to have recorded
    what was learned from Elk Head
another old man of the tribe . . . To transmit it
to the new youths
    the knowledge of the sacred pipe

"It is called a peace pipe, but now
there is no peace in the world" says Black Elk
"not even among neighbors, and from
what I've been told, there has not for a long time been any peace in the world"

The pipe is passed around.
    (Not only among men
    also inside men
    and also peace among the other creatures)
The Hut represents the universe and
the center pole, Wakan-tanka,
who holds up the universe.
The earth that she gave to men is red
the men who live on the earth are red
each red dawn a sacred event
  the earth, sacred
    and every step on it
      like a prayer.
The pipe is passed around
in the smoke the earth ascends, this great island,
the animals with four feet and the animals with wings.
The pipe is the universe; and it is man.
One smokes: and it enters into the center of the universe and into oneself.
Elk Head was talking
of the kinship among all the creatures of the universe
and the kinship between mankind and Wakan-tanka.
The tepee is the world
the fire inside the tepee Wakan-tanka,
who is at the center of the world.
    Nomads on the prairies, they put

Wakan-tanka's tepee in the center of the camp.
Also: the tepee is the universe and
around the tepee: the infinite, Wakan-tanka.
Poles of young willow trees
because as the leaves of the willow trees fall
and are reborn
so men die and come to life again.
He inhales the pipe and says:
"Let our brothers be gentle and not fear us."

The messages usually come in the shape of an animal
at times a very small one, an ant.
Animals are important, wise in their own right.
Black Elk says in an off-hand way:
        "It is no accident
that we have two feet like the birds."
The drum, round, is the universe. And its one-note sound
the beating of the heart of the universe.
The Sun Dance, with an eagle feather:
the feather, Wakan-tanka, who lives in the blue.
The Dance takes place in the full moon
        (the moon waxes and wanes, like our ignorance, that comes and goes).
The face, painted red: the red represents
all that is sacred, especially the earth
        from where the bodies come,
and to where the bodies return.
A black circle around the face
because Wakan-tanka is like a circle, she has no end.
There is much power in a circle
birds that fly in circles know this
        and their houses are circles
the coyotes who live in round hollows know this.

He said: "I was five years old when I began to hear voices.
Now I see everything from the peak of old age
bent over by these years as by a heavy snow:
        Many made into grass in the prairies . . .

It was in the Moon of the Strawberries (May)
and the *wasichus* found much yellow metal,
Crazy Horse was twenty and Red Cloud was the Chief.
My mother used to say: 'If you don't behave the *wasichus* will carry you off.'
"It was at the end of the Moon of Ripe Cherries (July)
and us children were playing the game of Knock-Them-off-the-Horse.
In my tepee I could hear the coyotes calling to the stars.
     My mother bent over the fire, roasting buffalo.
     My father arrives at night, on his shoulders an antelope.
"I see from my old age as from a lonely hill
       the stagecoaches in a circle
       our men going around in another circle
       closer and closer
       and then going around in two circles
       in opposite directions
       lying flat on our horses
          firing underneath their necks."

A leather half-moon,
     the moon represents all the things
that live and die.
They cut out another circle and they paint it red
and it is the earth. (It is sacred
because on it men place their feet
and raise their voices to Wakan-tanka.
She is of the family of mankind, they call her Mother.)
Blue Whirlwind breaks in: "The prayer
     a prayer of all things
because all things are really one.
We always see the sacred sky
and we know what it is and what it represents.
To know the four Beings of the universe
is to know that they are really One.
The sky is a shawl that enfolds the universe
and also enfolds the man who talks to Wakan-tanka."
And Black Elk adds: "Perhaps you have noticed
    that even though the breeze is very slight

you can always hear the voice of the poplar."

First (and most important) is peace inside you
when you feel your kinship with the universe
and you feel Wakan-tanka in the center of the universe
and that the center is everywhere and inside you
the second peace is between two men
and the third between two peoples
but there is none between peoples if there is none inside of man.

"In the Moon of the Yellow Leaves (September)
they signed a treaty with Red Cloud.
In the Moon of the Falling of the Leaves (October)
we camped near the Black Hills.
Much bison and we ate much meat and tanned much leather.
Crazy Horse wanted nothing to do with the *wasichus*.
In the Moon of the Birth of Grass (March)
there was a great council with the *wasichus*.
Crazy Horse and Sitting Buffalo did not attend.
Words and words and words: like a wind . . .
The Great Father in Washington wanted the Black Hills.
They would be like snow melting in the hands.
I was sad . . . It was so joyful to play there
and people were always happy in the Black Hills.
        And I remembered my vision
how I was carried there to the center of the world.
In the Moon of the Ripe Plums (August)
began the scattering of our people.
We burned the grass behind us
the smoke broad as the sky
        the glow broad as the night.
Sitting Bull went to Grandmother Earth (Canada)
Crazy Horse refused to leave the earth that was ours."

The ball, painted red (the color of the world)
with a blue circle (the color of the sky)
(Heaven and Earth come together in the ball)

the ball is very sacred, a little girl throws the ball
because she is new-come from Wakan-tanka.
She throws the ball in the four directions
because Wakan-tanka is in all directions.
The little girl's ball falls on the people
(like the power of Wakan-tanka on the people).
The buffaloes could not play this game
and they gave it to the two-footed ones.
The pipe goes round.
Brave Buffalo says: "One must have
a favorite animal. Study it
    know its movements and its sounds.
They want to communicate with man."
The pipe with red-willow bark.
    The great visions are for the whole nation.

"We learned in the Moon of the Falling of the Leaves
that the Black Hills had been sold.
One night, very cold, fire all night
I heard a little noise outside the tepee
I went out and it was a pair of porcupines
huddled together in spite of their quills
and we didn't scare them away because we were so sorry for them.
At the end of the Moon of the New Calves (April)
they took us to the fort. Crazy Horse surrendered
I saw him take off his war feathers
    he sat upon the ground.
They put us on islands to live like *wasichus*.
I did not tell anybody about my vision.
    I could not do anything because I was a child
    and not even Sitting Bull had done anything.
Lying in my bison-skin cloak I heard a coyote far off
I knew he was saying something, he wasn't saying words
    something clearer than words.
And strange news from the west:
Jack Wilson to the *wasichus* (but Wowoka was his name)
he saw the world all new, where everyone was alive

and the slaughtered bison ran again:
In the next Moon of the Birth of Grass
it would be the new earth, the return of the bison.
      The winter was very cold like a single long night.
The coyotes outside in the frozen night made me afraid.
And I remembered Crazy Horse.
In that Moon of the Snow upon the Tepee (December)
the *wasichus* killed the last of the bison.
No one knows where Crazy Horse is buried
     no matter: he is grass."

Lively Sparrowhawk says:
"Part of the plant goes up and welcomes the sun
and the other goes down seeking the water.
Wakan-tanka teaches the birds to make their nests
yet not all the nests are alike.
There are animals content with very bad houses
others have pretty ones.
Since I was a child I have observed the leaves of the trees
I have never seen two alike
if you look closely: there are little differences . . ."

And Blue Whirlwind:
"Some people prefer to be alone, away from the others.
With closed eyes many things can be seen
but these things are also distracting.
Some look for a hill, there they close their eyes.
Men are not enough, and one seeks an animal.
You can learn from animals' ways. For example:
horses get restless before a storm."
And again Brave Buffalo: "I was 10 years old
I asked the trees, the thickets.
     It seemed to me that the flowers were looking at me.
The muddy stones: some with faces like men
none of them answered me.
In a dream a round stone answered me
it said: Wakan-tanka.

It's curious: there are certain stones on high hills
round as the sun and the moon.
We know that all round things are relatives.
Those stones have stayed a long time looking at the sun.
I can't talk to Wakan-tanka, and I talk to stones."

And from Black Elk this prayer: "You placed
the four directions in the form of a cross.
The good road and the hard one you made them cross
and there where they cross the place is sacred."

Wounded Knee saw: bodies upon the snow
        a baby nursing at the breast of its dead mother.
From the summit of the mountain of old age
he sees again the bodies upon the snow
as clearly as he saw it all with young eyes, and he sees
that something else died there, in the mud of snow and blood
and was buried by that great snow that fell:
a very beautiful dream.
(And strange news from the west:
        under a rainbow tepees of clouds
many many camping in a great circle
around green grass happy horses
animals of all kinds on green hills
and the hunters came with game singing.)
        There was now no center anywhere.
        The sacred tree was dead.
Now he leaves his old voice on a recorder.

"When I was 20 in the Moon of the Yellow Leaves
I went off to the circus with Long Hair (Buffalo Bill)
to learn the secrets of the *wasichus*.
On the road-of-iron, to the great city
of lights so bright you couldn't see the stars
they told me they came from the power of the thunder
there I went like one who has never had a vision.
        I saw nothing that would help my people

they took things away from one another, the *wasichus*,
they didn't know that the earth was their mother."

He ended saying: "In these sad days
sad for my people
we are fighting each other for the ball
and some do not even take an interest in picking up the ball
this makes me weep.
     But soon they are going to pick up the ball
and the ball is going to come back to the center
and our people will be in the center with the ball."

And again, on the reservation:
     "There is no strength in a square"
(on the Pine Ridge Reservation
     in the square houses of the whites)
"You have seen that everything the Indians make is in a circle
and it's because the Mystery makes everything in circles
and all things try to be round
     the sky is round
and I have heard that the earth is like a ball
     the very strong wind goes in whirls
birds make their nests in the shape of a circle
because they have the same religion as we do
the sun and the moon swing in circles
and they both have a round shape
the seasons end where they begin
just like the life of man
our tepees were round like nests
and placed in the shape of a circle
now they have put us in square boxes."
     The vision was true, he says.
Almost blind. Surrounded by treeless hills.
(Not even a cloud)
"Great Spirit more ancient than all need,
than all prayer
     hear my fading voice!"

(Not even one cloud—
    the old men could not remember a greater drought)
"I send you my voice through a people in despair.
You told me that it would make the tree blossom.
With tears on my face Great Spirit
with tears on my face I come to tell you now
that the tree never blossomed!"
(The sky was still without a cloud)
"I am old, you can see, I went away and I did nothing. Here
in the center of the world, where as a child I had the vision
here I am again and the tree is withered.
Again, and perhaps this is the last time
I remember the vision. Perhaps a tiny root is living
feed it then if this is so, let it have leaves
and flowers and birds that sing.
Listen to me so that they may enter again into the hoop
and find the good road that is red
and the tree of the great shade!"
(In the sky, a few clouds
afterward a rain . . . a drizzle
    a muffled thunder)
The saintly redskin with tears on his face:
"In my sadness
hear me in my sadness
for perhaps I nevermore never again will speak:
        let my people live."
He fell silent. The tears smearing the paint
the tears and the rain smearing the paint
(soon afterward
    the sky clear again)

    The ball will come back to the center:
    and they in the center with the ball.

[D. D. W.]

THE LOST CITIES

At night, owls fly among the stelæ,
the wildcat snarls along the terraces,
the jaguar roars in towers,
a stray coyote howls in the Great Square
at the image of the moon in the lagoons
which in remote *katúns* were fish ponds.

Now, the animals are real
which in the frescoes were once stylized;
and princes now sell earthen jars in markets.
But how can one inscribe the hieroglyph again?
Again paint jaguars, and dethrone tyrants?
Rebuild again our tropical acropolis,
our rural capitals amid the *milpa* fields?

The jungle thickets full of monuments.
Altars in *milpas*. Arches
with bas-reliefs among the buttressed roots.
In jungle where it seems man never entered,
where only the anteater and the tapir
and the *quetzal* (still garbed like a Maya) go,
there lies an entire city.
When priests went up the Temple of the Jaguar
with jaguar capes, fans of *quetzal* feathers,
deerskin sandals and ritual masks,
shouting went up from the Ball Courts
with drumbeats, and the scent of copal incense
from the sacred chambers of *zapote* wood,
and the smoke of pinewood torches. . . . While underneath Tikal
there is another city a millennium older.
Today the monkeys howl on the *zapote* trees.

There are no names of generals on the stelæ.

In their temples and palaces and pyramids
and in their calendars and chronicles and codices
there is not one name of a leader or chief or emperor

or priest or politician or commander or governor;
nor did they record political events on monuments;
nor administrations, nor dynasties,
nor ruling families, nor political parties.
In centuries, not one glyph recording a man's name:
the archaeologists still do not know how they were governed.

Their language had no word for "master."
Nor a word for "city wall." They did not wall their cities.
Their cities were cities of temples, they lived in the fields,
among the palm groves and the *milpas* and the pawpaw trees.
Their temple arch was modeled on their hut.
Highways were only for processions.
Religion was the only bond between them,
but it was a religion freely accepted,
imposing no burden. No oppression.
Their priests had no temporal power
and the pyramids were built without forced labor.
At its height their civilization did not turn into an empire.
Nor had they colonies. Nor did they know the arrow.

They knew Jesus as the God of the Maize
and gave him simple offerings
of maize, of birds, of feathers.
They had no wars, nor knew the wheel,
but they had calculated the synodic path of Venus:
every night they noted the rising of Venus
on the horizon, over some distant *ceiba* tree,
as pairs of parrots flew homing to their nests.
They had no metallurgy. Their tools were of stone,
they never left the Stone Age, technologically speaking.
But they computed precise dates going back
four hundred million years.
They had no applied sciences. They were not practical.
Their progress lay in religion, mathematics, art,
astronomy. They had no means of weighing.
They adored time: the mysterious

effluxion of time.
Time was holy. Days were gods.
The past and the future are intermingled in their songs.
They used the same *katúns* for past and future,
in the belief that time was re-enacted
like the motions of the heavenly bodies they observed.
Yet the time which they adored abruptly ceased.
Stelæ remained unfinished,
blocks half cut in quarries
where they still lie.

Only lonely gum-tappers traverse the Petén today.
Vampire bats nest in the stucco friezes.
Wild pigs grunt in the avenues at nightfall.
The jaguar roars in towers—towers root-entangled—
far away in a distant square a lone coyote bays the moon,
and the Pan American jet flies high above the pyramid.
But will the past *katúns* one day return?

[R. P.-M.]

IN THE HALF-LIGHT

In the half-light
    (the gathering being clandestine)
smiling girls move from table to table
with olives and sardines
        Irene serves the wine
there aren't a lot of us
    one cup for all mouths present
one great loaf
    for all
        one song on every lip
    one song, and the one cup
we men exchange a kiss, the women kiss
there is a slave among us, there's Erastus
(city treasurer) the ex-rabbi Crispus
        and Titius Justus multimillionaire
grains of wheat scattered in the fields
        joined in a single loaf
scattered at well or barracks or shop
    we meet on Saturdays at twilight
separate grapes joined in a single wine
        Irene moves among the tables
and we talk together, reclining,
until midnight, beneath the orange torches
what am I saying? until the Sunday dawns.

There is one we do not see, the one who presides
    He who was put to death, crowned with vine-shoots,
yes, we dine round a dead man
    this being a funeral feast. He
celebrated thus before he died, that we
    might be thus drawn together in his absence
("do this in memory of me")
    and in this wine he lives.
Dawn comes. The lights grow pale.
    "Good-by, Irene"
and in the misty streets we scatter
    yet remain united.

[R. P.-M.]

COPLAS ON THE DEATH OF MERTON

Our lives are rivers
that go to empty into the death
that is life
Your rather funny death Merton
          (or absurd like a koan?)
your General-Electric-brand death
and the corpse back to the U.S.A. in an Army plane
      with that sense of humor so much your own you must have laughed
you Merton now corpseless dying of laughter
I did too
The Dionysian initiates used to place ivy
      (I didn't know Death)
Today I joyfully type this word "death"
To die is not the same thing as a car wreck or
                a short circuit
      we have been dying all our lives
Confined within our lives
      like the worm in the apple? not
like the worm but like
the ripeness!
Or like mangoes in this Solentiname summer
yellowing, waiting for the
golden orioles . . .
                the hors d'oeuvres
in the restaurants were never the same
as they were advertised in the magazines
nor was the verse as good as we wanted it to be
or the kiss.
We have always wanted something beyond what we wanted
We are Somozas always wanting more and more haciendas
      More More More
not only more but also something different
      The wedding of desire
the coitus of perfect will is the act
of death.
      We walk about among things with the air
of having lost a most important

folder.
   We go up in elevators and we come down.
We go into supermarkets, into stores
like everybody else, looking for
a transcendental product.
        We live as if waiting for an infinite
rendezvous. Or
     a telephone call from
the Ineffable.
And we are alone
immortal grains of wheat that do not die, we are alone.
We dream in steamer chairs on deck
  gazing at the daiquiri-colored sea
hoping that somebody will pass by and smile at us and
say *Hello*

Not sleep but lucidity.
   We move about in the traffic like sleepwalkers
     we pass by the lights
with eyes open and asleep
we sip a Manhattan as though asleep.
Not sleep
lucidity is the image of death
  of the illumination the blinding
radiance of death.
And it is not the Kingdom of Oblivion. Memory
  is the secretary of oblivion.
     She arranges the past in filing cabinets.
But when there is no more future but only a fixed present
all that we have lived comes to life again, no longer as memories
and reality reveals itself complete entire
in a *flash*.

Poetry too was a departure
like death. It had
the sadness of departing trains and planes
  Little Brenes Station

in Cordobita la Llana
the trains go by at night
"cante jondo" in the heart of Granada.
In all beauty, a sadness
and homesickness as in a foreign country
                    MAKE IT NEW
        (a new heaven and a new earth)
but after that lucidity
you come back again to the clichés, the
slogans.
Only at moments when we are not being practical
concentrating on the Useless.   Real Gone
only then does the world open up for us.
Death is the act of total distraction
also: Contemplation.

Love, love above all, an anticipation
of death
    There was a taste of death in the kisses
        being
            is being
                            in another being
                    we exist only in love
But in this life we love only briefly
and feebly
                We love or exist only when we stop being
when we die
        nakedness of the whole being in order to make love
                make love not war
        that go to empty into the love
        that is life

The city descended from the heaven that is not Atlantic City
        And the Beyond is not an *American Way of Life*
                Retirement in Florida
or like an endless *Weekend.*
Death is a door opened

upon the universe

        There is no NO EXIT sign

and upon ourselves

          (to travel—

   upon ourselves—

        not to Tokyo, Bangkok

          that's the *appeal*

      a *stewardess* in a kimono, *la cuisine*

continentale

that's the *appeal* of those Japan Air Line ads)

      A Wedding Night, said Novalis

It's not a Boris Karloff horror movie

And it's natural, like the fall of the apples

according to the law that attracts stars and lovers

There are no accidents

    just one more apple off the great Tree

you're just one more apple

Tom

         We leave our bodies as one leaves

         a motel room

But you're not Wells's *Invisible Man*

    Or like a ghost in an abandoned chalet

        We don't need *Mediums.*

And children know very well that death does NOT exist

that we are immortal

For can napalm kill life?

        From the gas chamber to nothingness?

   Or are the Gospels *science-fiction*?

Jesus entered the room and drove out the hired mourners

   That's why the swans sing said Socrates just

before they die

       Come, Caddo, we are all going up

            to the great Village

            to the great Village

Toward the place where all the buses and planes go

   And not as if to an end

   but to the Infinite

we fly toward life with the speed of light
And like the fetus breaking the amniotic sac . . .
Or like cosmonauts . . .

                                the exit
                                from the chrysalis

        and it's a *happening.*
the *climax*
of life   *dies natalis*
        this prenatal life . . .
The matrix of matter abandoned

                                Not an absurdity:
                                but a mystery
a door opened upon the universe
and not upon the void
        (like the door of an elevator that wasn't there)
And by now they are definitive.
        . . . the same as waking up one morning
            to the voice of a nurse in a hospital
And we no longer have anything we just are
        we just exist and we are mere existence
                    The voice of the beloved speaking
                    my love, take off that *bra*
The opened door
that nobody can ever close again
                "God who bade us live"
even though we long to return to
        atomic linkings, to
                unconsciousness.
                            And the bombs bigger and bigger.
Necrophilia: flirtation with death. Passion for dead things
        (corpses, machines, money, dregs)
and if they dream about a woman they picture her
in a car.
        The irresistible fascination with the inorganic
                Hitler was seen in World War I
                ecstatic before a corpse
                refusing to move

(soldiers or machines, coins, crap)
Gas chambers by day and Wagner by night
"5 millions" said Eichmann (it was more like 6)
Or else we want to put make-up on the face of death
The Loved Ones (don't say the dead)
made up, manicured, smiling
in the Garden of Repose of Whispering Meadows
    cf. *THE AMERICAN WAY OF DEATH*
  A Martini or 2 to forget his face
relax & watch TV
    the pleasure of driving a Porsche
       (*any line you choose*)
perhaps to wait for the resurrection frozen
in liquid nitrogen at −197°
    (put in storage like the grain that does not die)
until the day when immortality will come cheap
after coffee, Benedictine
a sport jacket to look young, to push death away
until they invent for us the serum of youth
    the antidote
for dying.
Like the good *cowboy* in the movies, who never dies.
  Looking in Miami for the Fountain of Youth.
After the advertised pleasures on the Virgin Islands.
Or on Onassis' yacht sailing on the Lethe . . .

You refused to be one of the men with a Name
and with a face that everybody recognizes in the pictures
in the papers
your desert that flourished like the lily was not that of
the *Paradise Valley Hotel*
    with cocktails at the pool
under the palm trees
nor were your solitudes those of *Lost Island*
  with the coconut palms bending over the sea.
LOVE? It's in the movies
    The eruptions of eternity

were brief
Those of us who haven't believed in the *Advertisements* of this world
    dinner for 2, *"je t'adore"*
       How to say love in Italian?
You told me: the
              Gospels don't mention contemplation.
Without LSD
but with the horror of God (or
    should we translate it rather as terror?)
  His love like the radiation that kills without touching us
and a void vaster than the Macrocosm!
  In your meditation you could see only that vision
  of the commercial plane from Miami to Chicago
  and the SAC plane with the Bomb inside
    the days when you were writing to me:
My life is one of deepening contradiction and frequent darkness
Your *Trip?* not at all interesting
    the journey to vast solitudes and extensions of nothingness
all as though made of plaster
              white and black, *with no color*
gazing at the luminous ball, blue and pink like agate
with Christmas on Broadway and copulation and songs
shimmering on the waves of the dusty Sea of Tranquillity
or the Sea of Crisis dead as far as the horizon. And
like a sparkling little ball on a *Christmas tree . . .*

    Time? *IS money*
it's *Time,* it's shit, it's nothing
    it's *Time* with a celebrity on the cover

And that ad for Borden's milk in the rain
years ago at Columbia, flashing on
and off, such fleeting flashes
    and the kisses in the movie theater
the films, the movie stars
so fleeting
    GONE WITH THE WIND

even though they still laugh beautiful and shining on the screen
the dead stars
    the car breaks down, the refrigerator
is going to be repaired
                       She was in a butter-yellow dress
                       orange-marmalade and strawberry-red
like a remembered ad in *The New Yorker*
and the *lipstick* smeared now with kisses
farewells at windows of planes that flew
        to oblivion
shampoos of girls more distant than the Moon
or than Venus
    A pair of eyes worth more than the Stock Exchange

Nixon's Inauguration Day is gone
the last TV image has dissolved
and they've swept up Washington
Time? Alfonso Time? Is *money* crap *shit*
time is *The New York Times* and *Time*
    And everything tasted like Coca-Cola . . .

    Proteins and nucleic acids
        "the beautiful numbers of their forms"
proteins and nucleic acids
        the bodies feel like gas to the touch
beauty, like a bitter gas
tear gas
    For the movie of this world is passing by . . .

        like Coca-Cola
    or copulation *for*
    that matter
Our cells are as ephemeral as flowers
        but not life
    protoplasms, chromosomes but
not life
    We shall live again the Comanches used to sing

our lives are rivers
that go to empty into life
now we see only through TV
then we shall see face to face
Every perception a rehearsal for death
beloved it is the time for pruning
All the kisses you couldn't give will be given
the pomegranates are in bloom
all love a *rehearsal* for death
So we fear beauty
When Li Chi was abducted by the Duke of Ch'in
she cried until she soaked her clothes
but in the palace she was sorry
she had wept.
The San Juan de la † is rounding the point
some ducks
swim by
"the uncanny isles"
or "desire" San Juan de la Cruz used to say
infinite desire
tears the fabric of this sweet encounter
and the Thracians used to weep at births says Herodotus
and sing at deaths
It was in Advent at Gethsemani when the apple trees
next to the greenhouse are like skeletons
with a blossoming of white ice like that
of the freezers.
I don't believe it Alfonso said to me in the Madhouse
when I told him that Pallais was dead
I think it's politics or
something like that.
Do they still bury a camel with them
for the journey? And in the Fiji Islands
clubs made of whale teeth?
Men's laughter at a joke is proof of their belief
in the resurrection
or when a child cries in the strange night

and mamma calms him
Evolution is toward more life
    and it is irreversible
and incompatible with the hypothesis
of nothingness
"Ivy Mara ey"
looking for it they traveled as far as the interior of Brazil
("the land where no one ever died")
    Like mangoes in this Solentiname summer
ripening
while the Novitiate is over there under a hood of snow.
        The golden orioles fly
    to Deer Island where they sleep
you used to tell me
It is easy for us to approach Him
We are strangers in the cosmos like tourists
    we have no home here only hotels
Like gringo tourists
      everywhere
cameras clicking even strangers
    And as one leaves a motel room
      YANKI GO HOME
One more afternoon dies over Solentiname
Tom
        these sacred waters sparkle
and little by little they go out
it's time to light the Coleman lamp
    all joy is union
    sorrow is to be without the others:
        Western Union
The cablegram from the Abbot of Gethsemani was yellow
    WE REGRET TO INFORM YOU etc. . . . .
I just said
O.K.
    Where the dead unite and
        with the cosmos are
            one

because it is "far better" (Philippians *i*, 23)
As the moon dies and is born again . . .
     death is union and
          one is now oneself
               one is one with the world
death is far better
the *malinches* in bloom tonight, scattering their lives
     (their renunciation is a red flower)
death is union
     ½ moon over Solentiname
     with 3 men
one does not die alone
     (their Great Meeting Lodge) the Ojibwas
and the world is much more profound
Where the Algonquin spirits with spirit moccasins
hunt spirit beavers over the spirit snow
     we thought the moon was far away
to die is not to leave the world it is
to plunge into it
you are in the hidden part of the universe
     the *underground*
outside the *Establishment* of this world, outside of time-space
without Johnson or Nixon
     there are no tigers there
                         say the Malays
(an island of the West)
     that go to empty into the sea
     that is life
Where the dead gather O Netzahualcoyotl
or "Heart of the World"
     Hemingway, Raissa, Barth, Alfonso Cortés
the world is much more profound
          Hades, where Christ descended
               womb, belly (Matthew *xii*, 40)
               SIGN OF JONAS
          the depths of visible beauty
where swims the great cosmic whale

filled with prophets
> All the kisses you could not give will be given

One is transformed.
. . . "as one was buried in one's mother's bosom . . ."
> a Cuna chief said to Keeler

Life does not end it is transformed
> another intrauterine state say the Koguis

that's why they bury them in hammocks
in the fetal position
> an ancient doctrine, said Plato

that off there in Hades there are
> people who have come from here . . .

Beziers, and the cathedral seen from the train
> Nothing of the yearned for has been lost
> > the smell of the south of France

the red Tower of Saint Jacques by the Tarn
the lights of Paris white and green, and those of the Eiffel Tower:
> *C-I-T-R-O-E-N*

Lax has traveled with circuses
> and he knows what it means

to strike the tent by lantern light
leaving the grounds deserted
and the truck ride by night toward another city
And when the wife of Chuang Tzu died
Chuang Tzu did not put on mourning
> Hui Tzu found him singing and dancing with

the rice pan for a tambourine
> the hammock is the placenta, the cord

of the hammock the umbilical cord
> "your headaches don't hurt you"
> > seed-plant-seed
> the dialectic of destruction
> > I mean

that of the wheat. To live
is to prepare for death and to give ourselves for the sowing of life
Until, masked and white-gloved, in comes
the agent

of what Acronym we do not know
And to deliver ourselves to death with love
And
if the stars do not die
they are left alone
if the stars do not return to the cosmic dust
     seed, plant, seed
death is union
     not in *Junction City*
Or as the Cunas also say
     "some day we want to eat a good meal"
And we clamor for the surrender of the beloved
And as Abbot Hezekiah used to say: it is
(the frequent thought of death) "as
when in the calm sea the fishes play
and the dolphins leap for joy"
     And, as the moon dies . . .
          They are on an island, they told Columbus
     in Haiti, they are all on an island
     eating mamey fruit by night
Or Boluto Island, west of Tonga,
happy and covered with flowers and spiritual breadfruit
"It seems he was electrocuted"
             Laughlin wrote me
"but at least it was quick"
          broken the veil
that divides the soul and God . . . And:
. . . because love yearns for the act to be very brief . . .
     the rivers of love of the soul
     go there to enter the sea
she arrived beautiful as Joan Baez in her black car
You used to laugh at the ads in *The New Yorker*
     well here's one for Pan Am
     Ticket to Japan
          To Bangkok
             To Singapore
     All the way to the mysteries

A ticket to contemplation?
    A ticket to contemplation.
                        And death.
    All the way to the mysteries
The commercial ads are
manuals of meditation, says Corita
                      Sister Corita
and ads of something more. Not to be taken
literally.
Biological death is a political matter
or something like that
    General Electric, the Parca
        a Vietnam *jet* for the corpse
but after this winter is gone, around Easter
or Whitsunday
you'll hear the Trappist tractors next to your cemetery
Trappist but noisy, turning over the earth
To sow, new Mayans, the ancient corn.
    The time of the resurrection of the *Caterpillars*
        and of the locusts
Like the banana tree that dies to give fruit the Hawaiians say.
    You were quite empty
        and having given all your love you had
nothing to give now
        And ready to go to Bangkok
in order to enter at the beginning of the new
to accept the death of the old
        Our lives
        that go to empty into life
the window of the great jet was weeping
        —as it took off from California—
    with joy!
At last you came to Solentiname (which wasn't *practical*)
after the Dalai Lama, and the Himalayas with their buses
painted like dragons
        to the "uncanny isles"; you are here
with your silent Tzus and Fus

Kung Tzu, Lao Tzu, Meng Tzu, Tu Fu, and Nicanor Parra
and everywhere; as simple to communicate with you
as with God (or as difficult)
        like the whole cosmos in a drop of dew
this morning on the way to the privy
Elijah snatched away by the chariot of cosmic energy
            and in the Papuan tribe when they saw the telegraph
            they made a tiny model of it
            so they could talk with the dead
The Celts used to lend money says Valerius Maximus
to be paid beyond the grave.

        All the kisses given or not given.
That's why the swans sing said Socrates
upon your chest the fan still
turning
        We love or are only when we die.
    The great final act the gift of one's whole being.
O.K.

[K. R. and M. J.-F.]

NOTE: *Jorge Manrique's* Coplas en la muerte de su padre *("Verses on the Death of His Father"), written in 1476, is one of the greatest poems in Spanish, a lament not only for the death of Manrique's father but for the passing of his whole era, the Spanish Middle Ages. In his* Coplas *Cardenal consciously echoes Manrique's opening lines: "Our lives are the rivers / that go to empty into the sea, / which is death."—D. D. W.*

LIGHTS, 1970–1985

NICARAGUAN CANTO

To the FSLN

During May the thrush sings in the morning
        when the rains are starting,
but toward evening in July, when the day's showers are over,
        the thrush sings sweetly and
in freedom, in the North. Later, the
trumpeting *zanate Cassidix nicaragüensis*
(a Nicaraguan bird) flies blueblackviolet
in October, or November, over Nicaraguan villages.
It is a proletarian bird: no glamor, always
found among the poor.
The "throat-cut bird" (red splash on neck)
        sings in the orchards.
The *toledo*, black velvet with a scarlet cap,
        sings TO-LE-DO TO-LE-DO where coffee grows.
The *pijul*, night-colored in its plumage, sings
        PEA-HOOL PEA-HOOL PEA-HOOL
        (and eats the ticks off cattle).
The beggar bird calls out
        TRES-PESOS TRES-PESOS TRES-PESOS.
The lesser oriole sings in the fields its tail tip-tilted
and every moonlit night the owl laments in cemeteries and ruins.
The "shrieker" of the River Escondido: always hidden
        one hears the shriek one never sees the bird.
           In the hills of Curinguás there are *quetzals*. . . .
In summer iguanas lay their eggs.
        Lizards are born in early winter.
Frogs begin to croak with the first rains in May.
        In June the thrush constructs its nest.
The alligators which have phosphorescent eyes at night
        lay their eggs in July
when turtles bury theirs along the beach
on moonless nights. Then come the storms. It is
the season of gales. Those heavy joyful downpours.
Called the "Just Judge" (from its song) the *justo juez*
        sings JUSTO-JUEZ JUSTO-JUEZ JUSTO-JUEZ

all through September on the barbed-wire fences.
                  And in September migrant swallows crowd the lake.
October: the fork-tail ducks arrive the swallows leave
assembling first on telegraph wires along the roads.
                  Crows pass through Matagalpa in November
and they return in May when the corn is young
                  to eat its tender cobs, a *campesino* said.
In December the odor of insecticide is in the air
         and in December the *zanates* lay their eggs
                  (their young hatch out in March, and there's
a clamor in their nests all summer up
         the palm trees).
In January the golden orioles begin to build:
neat golden nests suspended from *pijivay* palms;
                  they lay in February, and by
                           October their deserted nests are like
a village of thatched huts abandoned
to slow disintegration by the wind.
                  In February cedars flower
and the *buenos-días* sings on the Atlantic coast while nest building.
Oak trees in Solentiname bloom in March above the lake with
                  blossoms rosy as girls' lips.
And in summer: the *chichitote* sings the loveliest
                  song of any bird in Nicaragua
and the *cucurruchí* sings its name in summer nest building
while the shellfish are harvested in Bluefields Bay—
                  in March and April—and
in Ocotal, in April, the *quetzal* rears its young.

But another country found it needed all these riches.
To obtain the 1911 loans Nicaragua had to cede her customs rights
also the running of the National Bank
to lenders who reserved the right
to take it over. For those of 1912
she pledged the railroads also. On Feb. 2, 1911,
the banking group Brown Brothers & Co. acquired
an interest in us. Paying off one loan

meant setting up another, and
so on. (Once in there's no way out.)
          Bankers gathered round like barracudas.
    The Marines landed "to re-establish order"
and they stayed in Nicaragua for 13 years. Control
over railroads customs banks was not enough.
          Nicaragua sold her territory as well.
On 35 dollars a week Adolfo Díaz,
an Angeles Mining Co. employee, became the "capitalist"
of the "revolution" lending 600,000 dollars to the "cause."
The repayment of the Brown Brothers loan
          was underwritten with the customs revenue.
Corruption, national corruption was the bankers' banquet
          a buzzards' banquet
a ring of buzzard-gentlemen in morning coats.
Politicians: like blind bats hanging over us
          to shit upon us in the dark and piss on us
the shit and piss of bats as black as night
          black wings beating black air.
500,000 dollars more borrowed to stabilize the exchange
but—oh the bankers' banquet—
nor does the money even have to leave New York.
    The pledge involved placing the country in the bankers' hands.
The loan of 1911 was negotiated to establish
a National Bank which never left the foreign bankers' hands.
Brown Brothers went and bought what "paper" they desired
(I mean what paper money they desired) at 20 pesos to the dollar
while selling at 12.50, what paper they desired
which means that 20 pesos cost a single dollar (and they could
buy up as many as they wished) but when sold back
(which they could do at will) were worth one dollar sixty. I.e.
          they bought their money cheap to sell it dear
bought it from Nicaragua to sell it back
which pushed our prices up: corn, housing, education,
dances, railroad tickets.
          That was how the banker-mafia's looting worked.
    They attacked our national currency like gangsters.

And then the bankers lent the land its money back
at 6%.
The national revenues: collected by those foreign bankers
placed in a National Bank controlled by the same
foreign bankers, and distributed by the same foreign
bankers in association with the U.S. Secretary of State
(himself a shareholder of the Angeles Mining Co.).
Like the Honduran taxes taken up by Morgan
Morgan the fierce
        like the wild boar's slashing charge
           or the stench of puma on the wind.
Later even national territory was sold (under
the Bryan-Chamorro Treaty) for 3 million dollars
which also went straight into the foreign bankers' hands.
(Whereby the United States acquired exclusive rights
        over a Canal Zone 2 Caribbean isles
          one naval base
our country for 3 million dollars—the cash to the bankers—
the customs continuing in the lenders' hands for
an unspecified period—till all debts should be paid—
and the lenders have acquired the National Bank, likewise
the State Railroad where they bought a 51% interest for
1 million dollars more, until of all that once
made up the nation only the flag remained.)
        Dark night. The hut without kerosene.
       An owl hoots mournfully over the land.
The little *pijul*'s song is silenced.
There was no need for actual annexation financial
domination satisfied the States (with power over all presidents
from Díaz to the present incumbent) giving
all the advantages of annexation without the risks or the expense.
"Unless one simply plays with words"—a professor,
to the *Daily News*, in Paris, *ca.* 1928—
"nobody doubts that Nicaragua's independence
        is nonexistent."
To invest capital in Nicaragua and then protect
U.S. investments was the State Department's job.

Political expansion with a view to economic expansion:
economic expansion because capital did not produce enough
in the United States or not as much
as it could do in Nicaragua
THAT IS: imperialism namely
                interventions for investments or vice versa.
Diplomacy held the country in subjection through the bankers
and the bankers got the money out of Nicaragua by diplomacy.
            The mourning buzzards gathered round in morning dress.
Round Nicaragua's G.N.P.—
    just as sharks when they scent blood.
Internal disorganization and corruption fostered foreign
intervention consequently intervention fostered the
disorganization and corruption and developed them
        (that stares you in the face).
Whence, therefore:
imperialism as a disturbing and disrupting element etc.
fostering backwardness corruption etc. in Nicaragua: violating
treaties constitutions judicial decisions
        provoking civil war manipulating elections bribing
it has protected thieves prostituted politics impoverished the people
impeded union kept its agents in power against the people's will:
        thereby raised the cost of living defended
                oppression and brought death.
Thus Nicaragua (when Sandino appeared) found herself with
part of her territory alienated, the external debt
sky high, financial life entirely subject to
the group of New York bankers, and no progress.
            The whole country
as Cape Thanks Be to God is now: down to a single
line of huts, one street, and in it, six feet from the sea,
a buzzard squabbling over fish guts with a dog.

I said iguanas lay their eggs . . . It is the process. They
(or else the frogs) in the silence of the carboniferous age
                made the first sound
            sang the first love song here on earth

sang the first love song here beneath the moon
it is the process.
The process started with the stars.
New relations of production: that too
is part of the process. Oppression. After oppression, liberation.
The Revolution started in the stars, millions
of light-years away. The egg of life
is one. From
the first bubble of gas, to the iguana's egg, to the New Man.
Sandino was proud he had been born "from the womb of the oppressed"
(that of an Indian girl from Niquinohomo).
From the womb of the oppressed the Revolution will be born.
It is the process.
The male pelican puffs out his chest to court the female
before mating.
But the process still goes further:
Che smiling beyond death as though just back from Hades.

"Mahomet's Paradise" about which Gage spoke
I tell you Paradise has been sold up.
The Promised Land divided by *latifundistas*!
The land where I belong, just like
the *tigüilotera* dove or big-foot pigeon.
Nindirí, Niquinohomo, Monimbó
Nandaime, Diriá, Diriomo.
Ox of our youth which Darío once saw puffing vapor.
The clamorous peahens which we heard when we were lads.
The loud-mouthed swearing. We'd go to the river's mouth for clams.
The "cactus-hopper" in the cactus hedges.
Jays squabbling over mangoes, robbing nests.
Green parakeets along a branch, like shrieking leaves;
and when they rise you'd think the branch was flying!
There was a *curré* calling on a dry pole meaning drought.
5 p.m. and the handslap of *tortillas* being made
and the smell of the *tortillas* on the griddle
and the scent of woodsmoke. The hour
when the washerwomen return to Nindirí from the lagoon.

A flight of herons over Lake Managua.
The hour I'd go to meet my girl friend from the typing school . . .
    The hour when the first lights go on, and
    the last pairs of macaws fly homeward.
Managua: Rubén long-haired, with girl friend, on the quay
watching the white herons, and the brown.
    The evening breeze's soft caress.
            He with his "brown heron." The first kiss.
How often have we Nicaraguans overseas said over drinks
"ours is a land of shit"? In cheap hotels
where exiles meet, but then
we'd start remembering *tamales*, and tripe soup
    with coriander and wild chili peppers, the songs
to the Purísima in December (with the scent of *madroño* trees
    in bloom)
            the blue-blue lake and on the lake the flight
            of a heron like a white-white sail
        or the small sailing boat that's like a heron
and one began to think about
the scents of May: the warmth and smell of Nicaragua
    a rainy patio and the roof tiles wet
    tic tic tic tic tic tic tic tic
the small sound of water dripping off the roof
the whistle of the steamship *Victoria* as it draws near Granada
    a land—we said—deserving better luck.
And one has also thought about:
        windmills looking in the distance like iron roses,
        the song a railway engine sings in open country,
bringing the cattle home, milking early in the morning,
the smell of cheese in the cheese-women's boats
        a line of telegraph poles slanting across a meadow . . .
The *Victoria* at the quayside, or a TACA plane.
    A cottonfield in flower, looking like snow,
        a tractor working in it
                with the shape of Momotombo in the
                    background.
And the little diesel train to León which hugs the lake.

Or:

        Momotombo lit by the setting sun
           the lake all orange-yellow like the scales of a *mojarra*
     a youngster fishing in Mateare
                and the whistle of that León train.
Rubén always made the trip from Momotombo to Managua
in a little steamer. Watching the white herons,
and the brown. The lovely women. Sipping their cocktails
or cognac, he tells us, in the small saloon.
        Flowers provoked in him a feeling of voluptuous lassitude.
On a coffee plantation, a girl the color of chocolate
gave him clear water in a gourd. He saw the gourd was carved
        with shields, birds, letters, floral patterns, geometrical designs.
Masaya made him think of Hafiz: flowers in the gardens, flowers
in women's hair; the mayor had had the main street strewn with flowers.
Volcán Masaya: standing close to Nindirí. (In ages past, so Victor Hugo says,
Momotombo did not love Masaya's god because he was
so cruel.) Oh don't hit me . . . Oh don't hit me . . .
Ay mamita! Or you'll kill me . . . *Ay mamita!* His face
one livid mass. Nosecheeksforehead all one livid mass. The left eye
almost out. And the Major: Hit him harder . . . Hit him harder . . .
Kill him! Beating with the butt of his own carbine, bellowing:
Hit him harder! Harder! Harder! Kill the bastard! Kill . . .
He's got to die. The soldiers kept on beating
him with bundles of electric wires. He lay there naked
in the water trough. Hit him! Hit him harder! Go on hitting . . .
Kill . . . Kill . . . And then he took the wires himself.
And started kicking him. Right on the heart. You bastard, I'll
soon kill you (and the Major wound a steel wire round his neck).
The lad ran fifteen yards and fell. Left eye half out.
The right side of his face so swollen that it seemed to join
the neck. Dragged himself as far as the latrine. And died.
The body was thrown down the crater of Volcán Masaya:
the "Hell" of Masaya, as the Spaniards called it. Oviedo,
who had seen it: "In the deepest and the furthest part
of this great pit there was a liquid fire, of the consistency
of water, brighter than redhot coals; more fiery

than fire itself, if the expression be permitted;
and boiling, not everywhere but here and there,
the seething wandering from place to place,
with a continuous plopping bubbling sound from end to end.
According to the Indian headman Nindirí, at certain times
a naked wizened hag would rise out of the pit to tell
them whether they were going to win, or else that it was going to rain
and there would be much corn; and they threw in a man
as sacrifice: or perhaps two, or more,
some women maybe, and some boys and girls. But
since the Christians came that wizened hag
rose much less often. Indeed hardly ever. Saying Christians were
all evil and till they were gone she would not meet the Indians.
He added she was very old and wrinkled, breasts down
to her bellybutton; hair scanty and swept back; teeth long and sharp,
like those of dogs; skin far darker than the Indians';
eyes sunken, blazing . . ."
    For the Devil "was a murderer from the beginning."

Then there was Don Manuel Zavala, self-exiled in New York
since 20, saying at 75 that he would not return
to Nicaragua while the Gangster stayed in power
               (never calling him by name: just "the Gangster");
when a sick man he came back to his sisters' house, the Gangster
still in power; dying in his dear Granada, under the Gangster's rule.
Coronel knew an old man in Granada who said (who often said):
"I wish I were a foreigner, so that I could go home."
Or Gilberto who dreamed of emigrating, anywhere; to England
for example, "but with the Lake of Nicaragua, *zanates*,
the Granada-to-Managua train, pig's crackling with yucca, and
      Coronel Urtecho."

        Sails and herons on the deep deep blue.
      A lake the color of blue jeans, as William put it.
Such beauty was surely given us for love.
A launch out in midlake level with San Ubaldo . . .
        moorhens over toward Colón.

The lake by moonlight.
The moon above the lake, the water moon-colored.
So much beauty: for equality.
                (The lake on a calm night, and a motor launch a long way off.)
We'd go, the gang of us, to fish for *laguneros* and *guapotes*.
". . . the land which I shall give you . . . quoth Jehovah"
                And there are old sunken wrecks
which date back to the filibusters, or the Transit Company,
Vanderbilt's old paddle-steamers in which the sharks now breed
                perhaps with just the funnel showing
among the weeds and duck droppings. (Vanderbilt didn't even know
how to say Nicaragua. He said "Nicaragay.")
                The jetty at Moyogalpa rotted through . . .
The land is not a whore
        but now they've tried to sell her to a ghost
recluse in a hotel:
                        to the specter Howard Hughes.
The jetty at Moyogalpa rotted through
the black gaps which one had to jump by moonlight;
the launch which reached San Miguelito in the dawn:
they sold black coffee on the pier, and fried fish in *tortillas*
as the sun came up, with shades of green reflected in still water . . .
        A lad with a string of fish (the red and gold *mojarras*).
Land stolen from us.
Bankers, the Somoza dynasty, the Companies—they've
                stolen it, and steal it every day.
My homeland with its rivers, with my lovely rivers: huts
        with beached canoes and clothes hung out to dry
                latrines reflected in the water
and a rowing boat which heads downstream likewise reflected
cutting a sheet of glass
                        (a woman in it wearing red)
and the coffee-colored beachhen with
                lemon-yellow wings, spindle-shanked,
        deft stepping over the great water lilies
                                light as a flower itself.
The water is the hue of a *guapote*'s scales inshore

there where the yellow *sorocontil* blooms
                                a blue macaw in flight
a needle-duck swims past (snake-necked sharp-billed)
            a fast boat with an outboard motor passes
and an egret shoots out startled.
                The scent of cedar blossom.
                Hum of the sawmill by the river.
White herons at the edge each whitely mirrored.
        The new moon no broader than a slender heron.
It grows dark in the Escondido and the *cuaco* quacks.
                    Here we must build a country.
We stand on the threshhold of a Promised Land
                which flows with milk and honey: like a woman
                mel et lac sub lingua tua
the kiss comes when it should and in due course the kisses
"In the land which I shall give thee keep not thy brother illiterate
that he may gather in thy cotton and thy coffee. Quoth Jehovah."
            A land promised for the Revolution.
With all things held in common
        "as they were before the Fall of our First Parents"
I have seen green banana groves
            and sugar cane a different shade of green.
A meadow of *zacate* with some cows
                and the track leading on between *ocote* pines . . .
        I've dreamed of seeing art schools here
            and nursery schools.
I recall low ridges, yellow after burning,
            then plains with calabash trees and thornbushes.
A *pocoyo* hopping along in front of the jeep at night
                its bird's eyes gleaming in the headlights. I recall
coffee plantations at Telpaneca. Tobacco growing at Jalapa.
Jícaro, where
the Coco flows over gold dust and white sand.
        Beyond Jalapa the scent of balsam firs . . .
            Or, seen from a bus:
                a windmill, a small church
                on a hill, a country cemetery.

Macaws will always fly in pairs
and cross the evening sky gossiping (or squabbling)
                in macaw language.
I recall, though I don't quite know why,
        that little shop in San Rafael del Norte, after dark,
lit up, with a group of girls inside.
I saw mountains covered in pinewoods, with mountain pigeons cooing
and the song of "little widows." There
in the square of Quilalí hangs the propeller
                of a plane Sandino's men shot down
which now serves as village bell. And there
I heard the "little widows" sing their lonely sad lament.
And there Sandino dreamed of *campesinos* running great co-operatives.
(Beyond: the huts of the Miskito Indians begin,
on stilts along the Coco River, like birds' nests.)
Houses schools transport hospitals roads adequate food
hydroelectric plants
but at present just the beauty of arriving at a palm-leaf hut
when the mosquitoes start and the first star comes out
        we saw a jaguar's paw mark and we found the hut
had been abandoned.
        And the sadness of the evening, then, and the
                mosquitoes . . .
The Tuma! Oh to see the Tuma
country once again . . . Coffee in bloom, and corn.
        In March the cobs are tender.
Mist over the coffee plantations and, in the mist,
the whitish scent of coffee flowers (like that of orange blossom)
                with *chichitotes* singing
                and the "whistler."
                Campesino campesino
                what lovely fields you have!
                        it's a shame that capitalists own them.
        Or:
dark burnt fields (neat San José
de los Remates) with, beyond,
forests of cedar and lignum-vitae trees—and

       toucans calling.
And a "lion bird" (long-tailed and tawny as a lion)
going POON
      POON
         POON
The forests where the *quetzal* lives which cannot live when caged;
    the *quetzal*'s habitat, and that of Sandinistas.
        The Bijagual: a mountain in the North, up the Musún.
The Tapacucí, the Quiabú, the Tisey, the Tomabú: all mountains
in the area of Estelí.
        Pis-Pis, Condega, Yalí, Quilalí,
Yalagüina, Palacagüina
           Muy-Muy
         here we've dreamed of a land
     for which we've fought many battles
        so many battles
           (Pis-Pis: Pedrón was there, he seized the mines)
          and there is so much, brother, to be done . . .
Kukerawala River! Jaguars in heat roaring by moonlight
along its banks, and when they roar
        the monkeys shriek in fear.
        (We're going to build schools along the Kukerawala.)
        A just social system
which will ensure that the rule
        of social inequality does not return.
El Chipote: a damp
and misty mountain where the sun never gets through the trees,
with white-faced monkeys and macaws among the thickets: of *ocote* pine
sweet gums, mahogany with creepers and lianas, that's
     where "he" established his headquarters:
pocoyos screeching, jaguars roaring, toucans trilling.
High in its nest in the tallest of the liquidambar trees (at maybe sixty feet)
the *quetzal* sings its lovely territorial song; when still,
        you'd never see it, mimicking the light—
beneath a cloudy sky, its feathers are like leaves in mist;
but if the sun comes through it's iridescent, a
camouflage of sunlight on bright leaves. There

"he" was based: green clad, a wide-brimmed hat, red neckerchief . . .

Pearl Lagoon . . . Huahua Lagoon . . . and Sandy Bay . . .
Long sandbanks where beneath the moon
the Carey turtles come for love-making.
  Punta Gorda lighthouse at 100 feet above the sea.
   The Bay of Monquibel by Punta Mico.
And on these cays are coconuts. And on these coasts
are lobsters. The water blue, white cays
  (covered with white guano) lined with coconut palms.
Mico River. The Siquia. I can still see the dugouts—
  that's where the rubber-tappers go.
There too the brightly colored "dawn bird" sings.
League upon league of coconuts along the Atlantic Coast . . .
Canoes and motorboats which cut through glassy waters
   that soon revert to mirrors. . . .
A tiny village on a sandbank with a lonely lighthouse,
the surging of the waves, plop-plop of an electric generator
palm trees which sway in the sea breeze
   the moon behind the palm trees' silhouette.
The forest trees are felled in summer and the logs are marked
with paint or iron and dragged by tractor or oxen
to the gullies, to be swept down to the sea
by the first rains. I'd like to watch the lumberjacks at work.
To talk to turtle-catchers on the cays.
This is the land I sing. My poetry belongs here,
like the trumpeting *zanate*, or the wine-producing palm.
  I feel a longing for those eastern swamps.
  And grow nostalgic when I think of Prinzapolka.
The bay blue with a (banana) boat at anchor in the bay.
   Banana groves along the riverbank
    with plains behind
   lagoons like *quetzal* plumage
and then one reaches Sumo Indians' huts:
   a love song in the Sumo tongue, or in Miskito.
   And in those channels, sharks.

Ay la United Fruit!
Ay la Standard Fruit!
Companies have passed through here like cyclones.
There have been Sundays when Miskito girls
went naked to the (Baptist) church
Miskito girls who had no clothes to wear.
And people have quite literally died
of hunger here.
                              Brother Pedrón Altamirano!
When I think of the sad light of miners' lamps
I see the gold which travels down a side stream of the Prinzapolka
going on its way to vaults of Wall Street banks.
It's Wall Street that the "sun bird" sings against in Prinzapolka!
          The struggle was a national one, Sandino said
                    adding that it would be international one day.
In Mr. Spencer's gold mines they X-ray
each miner twice a year
to see if he shows symptoms of TB.
If there's a shadow, he's paid off
at once. In due course he spits blood, and tries
to claim: "In good health when dismissed"
he'd caught the disease later. No, the mine
is not responsible. And so he dies on a Managua sidewalk.
(If he is a Sumo or Miskito Indian he goes home, infects
his village. Whole villages have been wiped out this way.)
Companies have stripped the Coast like locusts:
bare stumps where pinewoods used to stand.
Nothing will ever grow where they have been.
Here Magnavox passed through.
          Attracted by the scent of raw materials.
In the words of that president of General Motors
"what's good for General Motors is good for the United States"
and vice versa.
     Imperialism says it wants to make us happy!
Great forests on both banks, and in between
          the river like another (liquid) forest.
Suppose it's a Miskito settlement that we have reached

and a Miskito love song that we hear, with the word love
     kupia-kumi = "one-single-heart."
"One-single-heart": the military and money look like that
today (but those two have no heart). No: the sole true *kupia-kumi*
is Love, namely the union of the people to achieve
the Revolution. Only Love is truly "single-heart."
Not: Caribbean Bener Lumber Co. Bluefields Lumber Co. Gold
Mining Co. Luz Mines Ltd. American Smelting & Refining Co.
Neptune Mining Co. Long Leaf Pines Co. Cukra Development
Co. Nicaragua Lumber Co. the list seems endless
Magnavox the list seems endless
                             General Sandino
        the Marines are at the hut!
at the hut to rape the girl!

You brother walk unshod but you own tungsten.
Illiterate brother with antimony mines.
        I.T.T. is on the prowl
     like a jaguar seeking whom it may devour.
          (That's as certain as
that General-You-Know-Who likes raping little girls
more *campesinos* get chucked out of helicopters
         Monsignor Chávez still keeps blessing the régime!)
Did someone say the Minister of Economics would protect
his people, rather than Esso?
                  The *encomienda* system still survives.
And when the bell rings daily to halt dealings
on the New York Stock Exchange you can be sure that they
     have taken something from you brother which you did not even
know was yours. When Wall Street dealers say: "We dropped
five million cash this afternoon"
     that means in Wall Street parlance that they bought
five million dollars' worth of stocks and shares.
Secretaries of State may come and go like migrant birds
but Standard Oil remains.
The Canadian said to the Miskito: communism is bad
it takes all that we own. And the Miskito (who listens to Radio

Havana in Miskito) answered: bad for you, got everything
        good for Miskito
                he not got anything.
                It would be international one day
Sandino said. He also used to tell the *campesinos*
"One day we are going to win. Should I not see it
the little ants will come to tell me in my grave."
Darío prophesied, triumphantly received on coming home,
a yet more glorious country, in a toast to youth, poor good Rubén:
"I drink to lasting victory for this land of ours" . . .
(that was in 1910, the next year—1911—saw
the coming of the bankers).
        The fight is with us still: Sandino versus the Marines.
How many chopping brushwood in the hills might match Darío?
Hut dwellers in perpetual night.
        The bootblack who might have been a great philosopher.
The goatherd a great painter. Not only
                just not knowing how to read or write:
                        not even how to think, wish, dream.
See those buses laden with the poor? They're the true owners
        they put up the Bank of America building—
who the hell knows how tall—and they (who else?)
the bridges and the reservoirs. All they need do is take things over.
                The poor. Above all
                the very very poor
("that fucking load of stinking shit-eaters").
A flight of jets stains the blue sky, and don't you know
that they've excluded you from civilization, brother?
yet it's your lemon grass which gives—though you don't know it—
the citronella which those jets require.
Your golden hardwood used to make truck floors
your lignum-vitae for propellers pulleys and . . . Oh well . . .
        Play me this song on your guitar
                Things do matter
                but people matter more
One suddenly comes on the camp, beneath mahogany
and ceiba trees: huts. With fireplaces, and earthenware

jars, stones to grind corn, beds of rawhide, strips
of salted meat, a carbide lamp in front of a St. Anthony,
calabashes closed with corncob stoppers, a young child crying
in a sisal hammock with bright-colored tassels,
the sounds of a victrola, and a guitar,
Sandino reading *Don Quixote*, in the open air, by firelight.
      The camp remote as any *quetzal*'s nest.
Now Sandino is back on the Chipote once again, *muchachos*.
      Once more attacking Telpaneca in the night.
Pedrón once more down by the Coco
                unless he's near Boaco.
Again the peasants leave cornstalks unsnapped
           black kidney beans unthreshed
to join Sandino and besiege the mines rout the Marines
set fire to Standard Fruit Co. offices.
      A misty night without a moon: one
hundred and forty Sandinistas take the sentries by surprise . . .
Or Sandinistas lying in evening ambush on the track
down which Marines will come:
              Miguel Angel Ortez looms up in the night
black-trousered with a head of long fair hair
rifles machetes 2 old-style Lewis guns and shouts of
VIVA SANDINO! (between shots) and PATRIA LIBRE O MORIR!
The mist dissolves, no Sandinistas there . . .
One evening when the Marines were just about to enter a pine forest
      (and they did hear the throb of a guitar through trees) . . .
A sudden challenge in San Rafael del Norte from the guard post:
"Halt, who goes there?"
"Friend! Long live Nicaragua!"
"Advance and give the password friend!"
"Thou shalt not sell thy country!"
Pedrón joins forces with Ortez again to fall on Jinotega
Pedrón going from village to village once again to say "Don't use
your vote!" After one ambush the Marines could hear good-byes
mules trotting carts that clattered off into the night
but Lee fell wounded . . .
      Soon: *campesinos* running great co-operatives

the campaign against illiteracy
and youngsters from Muy-Muy will get their ballet school
theatres in Tecolostote, in Telpaneca. How clear the vision
of a land where exploitation
is abolished!
The country's wealth shared equally
the total G.N.P. an equal share for all.
Nicaragua without the National Guard, the new day beckons!
A country without fear, with no dynastic tyranny. Sing loud, *zanate*
sound your bugle call.
No beggars   no prostitution   no politicians
It's clear there can't be freedom so long as some are rich
so long as some are free to exploit others, free
to steal from others
so long as there are class divisions there's no freedom.
We were born neither to serve our fellows
nor to hire them
but rather to be brothers
each born to be a brother to the others.
Capitalism: men buying/selling men what else?
What kind of journey brothers can we take
while some still travel First and others Third?
There is nickel waiting for New Man
mahogany waiting for New Man
thoroughbred herds waiting for New Man
the only thing still lacking is: New Man.
Come *compañeros*
tear down the barbed-wire fences.
Break with the past. Because the past was never ours!
. . . those who'd still live off brothels.
As that girl said, in Cuba: "The Revolution
is above all else a matter of love."
I'd like to see billboards by the roadside here:
Your worth lies not in what you take
from others but in what you give
—2 a.m.: San Rafael del Norte, thickening mist,
Sandino going to the church with six companions

to marry Blanca. He with pistol riding-boots red neckerchief.
Blanca in white, with veil, and coffee blossom garland.
The groom went back into the hills through mist and coffee plants
    in flower.
                Those were the days when people sang
                    The buzzard is already dead
                    they take him to his grave
Each tree, each bush, each rock could suddenly
        turn out to be a Sandinista sniper.
(Hunger isn't just a matter of tortillas and black beans
        although it's *also* a matter of tortillas and black beans.)
And a poster saying
    that those who died for the people
    are gloriously risen in the people.
What does the "throat-cut bird" proclaim, or the Just Judge,
perched on the barbed-wire fences? A new dawn
and new production contracts.
           From each according to his ability
              to each according to his needs.
A system which understands and meets the needs of life
    production determined by the needs. Example:
clothes made not in order to make money, damn it,
        but in order to clothe people.
And all luxury homes will be expropriated
        all those incapable of work
shall have their needs met by the state
                (*The Tupamaro Program*)
Words of the *Popol Vuh*: "Let all the people rise!"
There's so much corn to plant so many kids to teach
    so many sick to cure and so much love
to give and so much song.   I sing
a country waiting to be born. The lake part blue, and partly
        silver partly gold. A flight of herons
            in the sky
"in truth it flows with milk and honey" (said the explorers)
and Jeremiah later: "Tell it to the islands
and in the dance teenagers shall rejoice"   (Jer. 31: 10–13)

Our own New Men.
Our own New Men are all we lack.
          ("Ye shall enter the Promised Land but yet not all
                    shall enter")
Communism or the Kingdom of God on Earth which is the same.
General Genie's "interrogation" chambers shall become
rooms where little girls may play with dolls
and small boys with Pinocchio
          tanks turn into tractors
and police vans into high school buses
     and the machine will then be man's best friend.
General of The-Free-Men
          the little ants will come to tell you in your grave!
     What days those days when boys shall have Pinocchio
(and when my dream comes true there'll be no rich)!
Let's go and write this slogan on the walls
          LIFE IS SUBVERSIVE
or else

          LOVE IS THE AGITATOR
or the last words of Leonel Rugama (guerrillero) to the Guard
     SURRENDER?   ME?   UP YOURS!
or write these lines by Pasos on the walls
          Go home, go home, go home,
          Yankee, go home, go home!
When a *curré* calls on a dry pole that means drought
     but when he calls on a green one rain is near.
Tear down those fences and
let all the people rise, even the dead.

This is the land of which I sing.
Hoarsely, like the *guardabarranco*
     which at a distance sounds just a bit like cattle lowing,
he builds his nest in holes in rocky canyon walls.
And like the cheerful *güis* in Nicaragua's parks and orchards
the *cierto-güis* which keeps repeating CIERTO-GÜIS
     or like the *guas* in Chinandega and Chontales
which sings in the dry fields, announcing rain

thus too my song. . . .
And like the "lion bird" (or *cocoroco*) a lonely fellow
    which sings in anguish to announce a puma.
And like the "clock bird" singing out the hours
or the Atlantic "sun bird" saying that dawn is here
thus do I sing. . . .
And I sing like the bird they call "swamp-snorter"
(because it snorts in marshes and in swamps)
but also clearly, like *zanates* bugling
        zanatillo zanatillo
           the bird of the oppressed—
or like the "creaker" (grating in damp woods)
or like the *ché-ché* of the northern hills (guerrilla hills)
        which sings CHE-CHE CHE-CHE CHE-CHE
and like the "happy bird" whose song means FEELING JOY
the poet's voice sings FEELING-JOY
                JOY   JOY
And I am also like the sad *cocoyo* at twilight
        so sadly singing SCREW-THEE-TOO
or *tecolotes* (owls with enormous spectacles)
        which hoot among the ruins.
Or like the *pijul* which, when rain is near,
      sings out PEA-HILL PEA-HILL PEA-HILL
among the *sorocontil*'s yellow flowers on the San Juan
near Coronel Urtecho's farm   PEA-HILL PEA-HILL
      (announcing rain)
or like the "six-o'clock bird"
        which sings a sad song in the wilderness
but only at 6 o'clock each afternoon
          when it will not stand out
    thus too my song.
Or like perhaps the loveliest bird on earth:
the *quetzal* of the misty forests—
      yet more lovely in the sunlight than the shade—
its alarm note is a harsh CRACK that's audible for miles
its territorial song is a melodious (2-tone) whistle
      it repeats

and repeats.
To give A.P. the lie (and U.P. too)
        that also is the poet's task.
"Like certain birds which only sing for certain races"
as Joaquín Pasos said.
               There are
               problems
               only when
               there are solutions
"One-single-heart"
            PEA-HOOL PEA-HOOL PEA-HOOL
                                    PEA-HILL
     JOY JOY
                  CRACK!!!
    I-SEE-THEE
                           GO-LAY GO-LAY
        SCREW-THEE-TOO   SCREW-THEE-TOO
      CHE CHE
   MARY DAWN IS HERE / MARY DAWN IS HERE

                                       [R. P.-M.]

The coronation ceremony was in Belize this time,
the king riding on a white horse in procession to the church
with the uniform of a British major, the others on foot
with red frock coats (castoff) of British officers
of all ranks and wearing sailor pants.
His Majesty was placed on a seat next to the altar
and the coronation rites were performed by the chaplain
acting on this occasion as the Archbishop of Canterbury.
When they reached the part that says: "And all the people said:
'May the King live forever, long live the King'"
the frigates shot off their cannon, and the Indian
and black vassals shouted: "Long live King Robert!
God save the King!" His Majesty meanwhile
seemed absorbed in looking at his lace. After the anointing
he kept touching with his finger the holy oil (which was
castor oil) and then putting his finger to his nose
but he did not flee in the midst of the ceremony to climb a coconut tree
as his illustrious ancestor had done in Jamaica.
After the ceremony the crowd
went to the schoolhouse for the gala banquet
in which no food other than rum was served
until King and court rolled dead drunk on the floor.

Vanderbilt never in his whole wretched life had had a vacation
and this time he determined to have one in Europe and therefore
a special ship was built. No one had ever seen anything
more fabulous on earth. The newspapers were stunned.
No private yacht could be compared with the *North Star*
in size or luxury: 2,500 tons; 300 feet long;
enormous paddle wheels moved by two motors. And the
walls of the vast saloons: of marble and granite.
The coffered ceilings of rosewood and sandalwood; in the ceiling
medallions of American heroes; the staterooms
like the apartments of Cosimo de'Medici
(even though his carpet in Washington Place was frayed)
and with a great cargo of ice, wines, rare foods, famous
chefs from New York, and a chaplain who blessed the food.

This time Vanderbilt "spent without his usual inhibitions."
In London the *Daily News* saluted the floating palace
with an editorial. He was given a reception in Mansion House
with many flunkies and with Carlyle. The Lord Mayor drank a toast
to "Mr. Vanderbilt the foe of monopolies" and Vanderbilt
made a speech—the only time in his life that he did so.
He saw Victoria and Prince Albert only at the Opera.
But in Russia Czar Alexander lent him his carriage
and Grand Duke Constantine, his son, inspected the ship
and asked permission to make a sketch of it. Emperor Napoleon (Louis)
paid him no attention because he was busy with the Crimean War.
They did not open the Tuilleries for them and Mrs. Vanderbilt
did not see the wardrobes of the Empress Eugenie. Summer on the
Mediterranean . . . King Bomba of the Two Sicilies . . . then
Greece, etc., and the millionaire got bored and went back home.

But the British agents got screwed because the monarch
began to sell great portions of his kingdom
for barrels of rum.
In 1839 the sovereign "in the fourteenth year of his reign"
(having already sold a third of Nicaragua
half of Costa Rica
and a limitless stretch of Honduras)
was forced by McDonald to make his will
naming McDonald and others as "Regents"
in case His Majesty should die before the Heir Apparent
came of age
and shortly after this the King was kind enough to die
and his Eminence Colonel McDonald published a decree
in the name of the child king George William declaring
". . . the said surrender of territories null and void . . .
because the grantees obtained them at a time when the king
was bereft of reason [drunk]." But the decrees of one king
were worth as much as those of another, and one Shepperd, an old
British sailor, almost blind, in his Greytown house (San Juan del Norte)
years later still kept in a cupboard those old papers, with
        "X his mark"

(because the sovereign couldn't sign)
of King Robert Charles Frederick,
that made him the owner of a third of the Mosquito Kingdom
("We, by our special grace, do give and grant . . .")
from Bluefields Bay to Colombia (Panama)
a total of twenty-two million acres
and a Texan named Kinney, who speculated in cattle and enormous
chunks of Texas, acquired the moth-eaten papers of the
sea-wolf through the promise of a half million dollars
(the biggest real-estate speculation in his whole life)
and he organized a so-called Central American Company
with authorized capital of $5,625,000 and 21 directors
and two hundred twenty-five thousand shares at $25.00 a share;
each share would bring 100 acres of land
on being presented at the company office in Greytown.
On Wall Street they believed he was a partner of Walker
but he was more a rival.
"I have land titles to begin legally," he said.
"I'm going to create a government and the rest is easy."
President Pierce, it was said, was on his side.
But the "Transit Company" was not . . .

In New York he recruited 500 men to capture Greytown
but before he could do it he was shipwrecked opposite Greytown
he reached Greytown shipwrecked and bankrupt to boot
with only 13 men and a printing press that he saved from the wreck.
But even so he had himself elected civil and military governor
by the handful of lazy inhabitants, in "a democratic election"
and he organized a provisional government while they were drawing up
the new constitution inspired by that of the United States.
Ten days later the press began to publish
the newspaper (bimonthly) *The Central American* with ads
for commercial firms in Greytown, import & export houses,
hotels, schools, bars, lawyers, banks,
clubs, doctors, bookstores, nightclubs, etc., etc.,
to attract immigrants. Alsop & Co., on California Street
(Buy and Sell Exchange) . . . Benicia-Boarding School

for young gentlemen—*The Atlantic Loan & Security Bank*
        The Ocean House (. . . on a romantic Lagoon . . .)
CAFE FRANÇAIS (every kind of refreshment)
to attract immigrants to that place which was nothing but
a swamp with 50 houses (thatched roofs) and 300 inhabitants
of all colors, nearly all blacks (ex-slaves from Jamaica,
fugitives from justice, and an occasional European) on the shore of a
noxious lagoon, full of alligators and surrounded by the forest,
a place that had been described as "one of the saddest
and most desolate on earth . . . so much so that, however varied
the experiences that the traveler had had with lugubrious places
the memory of Greytown would stay with him
as among the most melancholy and dismal . . ." The only banks
were sand banks covered with shark bones
that obstructed the sea view. The lively dance halls,
the lively dance halls of *Delmonico's* (open till dawn)
were probably the frog-filled swamps.
The monkeys: perhaps they were the music at *Mike's*
("Visit Mike's—The Best Restaurant"). Language Schools:
the cockatoos! *The Green Resort* perhaps wild boars
and tigers. Royal Caribbean with its enchanting singers
the Jamaica Grill, Jimmy's Café, so many more puddles
(or the luxurious St. John) with crocodiles, with mosquitoes
("Make your reservation . . .") but the immigrants did not arrive.

Vanderbilt had given up the presidency
of the Transit Company when he went to Europe
and he had made Morgan president and while he was traveling
Morgan and Garrison had made the shares fluctuate
earning enormous sums at Vanderbilt's expense
and he (who said "I don't give a shit for the law,
I've got the power") when he came back just sent them a note:
        "Gentlemen: I will ruin you. Sincerely Yours,
            Cornelius Van Derbilt"
The Transit Company had never paid Nicaragua
the 10% of the profits claiming that there weren't any profits
and Nicaragua couldn't claim that there *were* profits

because of the peculiar way the company kept its books,
which consisted of never recording either passengers or cargo.
Toward the end of December '56 the bar of the Hotel St. Charles
in New Orleans had more noise and more cocktails
than usual because the steamship *Texas* was leaving
with recruits for Walker toward the lands of the sunny South,
the hot, sensuous South, with the laudable intention
of robbing them (but those who went to Nicaragua almost never came back)
Italians who fought in Novara, Prussians
from the campaigns in Holstein, Englishmen from the Crimean War,
Yankees from the expedition to Cuba . . . (They carried the rifles in boxes
shaped like coffins.) And on the very same seas of Kidd and Morgan—
the other Morgan, the pirate—they would scan with their telescopes
the western, wood-covered coast of Cuba
saying that it would "sooner or later belong to Uncle Sam."
(And when they got to Nicaragua they would open the coffins.)
Morgan and Garrison who were losing control of the company
courted Walker so that he would confiscate it from Vanderbilt
who had never paid anything to Nicaragua, which now belonged to Walker,
and would deliver to the two partners the dead corporation with
a new contract that would set them up as a new company.
A plan of unscrupulous captains of industry against
a rival equally unscrupulous. A shark fight
like those of the reef of San Juan del Norte. There was stupor
on Wall Street when they learned of Walker's confiscation.
Panic among the investors. They all rushed
to sell their shares. On January 1st they had been at 18,
on February 14th at 23¼. On March 14th (when
the news arrived) they went down to 19, and on the 18th, to 13.
In 4 days 15,000 shares changed hands. Vanderbilt, wounded,
attacked Walker. Oh, the bastard, said Vanderbilt
I'm going to screw Walker. No more boats to Nicaragua.
And as Morgan and Garrison weren't ready with theirs
the filibusterer with the grey, empty eyes ("that in daguerrotypes
seem to be without eyelashes") and a mouth that under no circumstances
did anyone ever see smile, was left trapped in Nicaragua.

The immigrants didn't arrive. And the British agents
didn't recognize the "provisional government," and besides
Walker was now in control of Nicaragua, and Kinney had no funds anymore
and besides he was ill, and many of his followers
went off with Walker. For some months he vegetated in Greytown.
Then he went away sick and without one cent.
              Sick and penniless.

Afterward Vanderbilt sold his ships and snapped up railroads,
              and forgot about Nicaragua.
His wife asked him: "Aren't you rich enough?"
        "Not yet."
Just about then a newsboy ran by under his window on
Washington Place shouting: CIVIL WAR!

The newspaper from San Juan del Norte with its fantastic ads
is disintegrating in the Library of Congress in Washington,
the librarians say, and it can't be xeroxed; you touch it
            and it turns to ashes.

[D. D. W.]

That afternoon I thought I was still on my Solentiname island
and not peering out a plane window over New York Harbor.
Ships down below, barely moving, my plane just as slow.
     The rush-hour traffic jam at Kennedy Airport
forced us to circle over New York for an hour.
What miracle has put me above Manhattan this late afternoon
circling skyscrapers reddened like the clouds?
From the seat beside me (vacant) I picked up a *New Yorker*
"This week Washington awoke from its Watergate stupor."
Senator Fulbright fears they may fall into a totalitarian system.
Ladies and Gentlemen: Kennedy Airport is still jammed up.
As I press against the window bent over the water of New York Harbor
     the plane, as if anchored to a cloud, doesn't move.
Ad for an island—swimming pool tennis cottages water sports
     The Island Company Ltd., 375 Park Avenue
Cartoon of a fat man with a newspaper saying to his wife
"All these years of struggling and the *Times* is *still* calling me a
     'reputed Mafia leader'"
Ladies and Gentlemen . . . we've now been picked up by radar and
we're heading straight for Kennedy Airport on automatic landing
factories, trains, little suburban houses all alike, matchbox cars,
and finally on the runway. Along with a hundred more planes like sharks.

Waiting for me was young, bearded Gerard, who miraculously
brought me to New York and tells me to call him Tony,
we're riding in his poor old car toward New York, rivers of cars,
he invited me to a benefit for the Managua victims
but he needed someone to pay the fare, he says.
     He finally got it, God takes care of everything. He works
with orphans, drug addicts, poor Puerto Ricans
and while he was in a ghetto, he got the idea of a benefit for Managua
he needed a hall, was turned down at Columbia, looking up at the sky
he saw the Episcopal Cathedral of St. John the Divine, walked in
     and the Bishop said to him, "Why not?"
     New York prisoners gave pictures they painted
     North American Indians also gave woven things and ceramics
more rivers of cars trains trucks, superhighways all crisscrossing

he's a Catholic he tells me and also a Zen
he'd worked before at St. Patrick's Cathedral, he couldn't stay on there
            its present cardinal worse than Spellman
along the highway messages from gas stations drive-ins motels
        a car graveyard melancholy in the twilight
some hippies have camped in the Gethsemani monastery, he says
guys with girls too, the abbot allowed it
in the United States monasteries are getting emptier and emptier
young people prefer small communes. I tell him
that Merton used to tell me those orders would disappear
and only small communes would be left
                the sky smog and ads
                    rectangular hulks among the exhaust fumes
and most all the contemplatives, Tony says, have a mentality that's
bourgeois   middle-class
indifferent to the war issue. And to the Revolution.
            LIQUORS   DRUGSTORE
"You think New York's changed a lot?"
I was here 23 years ago. I say: "It's just the same."
        The rows of red and green traffic lights
        and the lights of the taxis and the buses.
            "Madison Avenue" says Tony. And laughing:
"It's funny: Ernesto Cardenal on Madison Avenue." And I look
at the deep canyon, the sunken gorge of buildings
where *the hidden persuaders* hide behind their windows
        selling automobiles of True Happiness, canned Relief (for 30¢)
            The Coca-Cola Company
we cut through the canyon of windows and trillions of dollars.
"For centuries they didn't eat meat; now that many of us are vegetarians
they're eating meat" he says. From a street corner the Empire State
        (just its bottom floors). At the heart of Imperialism.
"Famous monks come to lecture on asceticism and
        they stay at luxury hotels." And now on the West Side
        Cafeteria—Delicatessen—Dry Cleaning
We arrive at Napoleon's apartment, 50th and 10th Ave.
Along the sidewalk, blue-jeaned and blue-eyed teenagers
clustered around bicycles or sitting on the stoops.

The doorbell doesn't work but Napoleon and Jackie were expecting us.

Napoleon Chow of Chinese and Nicaraguan ancestry
and Jackie is an anthropologist, a specialist on Turkey.
The little apartment monastic, but with Persian tapestries.
I call Laughlin at his home in Connecticut.
Surprised: "What the devil am I doing in New York?"
He laughs clear from Connecticut. He'll come in on Saturday so we
    can see each other
at his place in the Village.
Napoleon and Jackie do yoga. On many days they fast
completely, other days they cook very well, eating
        Chinese, Turkish, Nicaraguan food
("food as joy; sacrament")
There is an Angora cat that shits in the toilet just like people.

Tuesday evening, the Cathedral of St. John the Divine
110th Street, opened its bronze doors for the exhibition.
    I read my "Oracle over Managua" (the Earthquake part)
among prisoners' paintings and Indian ceramics.
A full-bearded rabbi prays: "Our guilt
in such tragedies . . ." And the Dean of the Cathedral: "Our System,
Lord, which aggravates those catastrophes . . ." (And I'm thinking:
    the Somozas
        a 40-year-long earthquake.) Benedictine Brother David:
"And Lord it is in New York of all places
where you gather us from different countries and religions
to pray for Managua, and to meditate
    on how much ought to be destroyed here"
Dorothy Day was ill so she couldn't come.
María José and Clemencia, two beautiful Nicaraguan girls (I met
    their father)
ask me how those streets were left (I met him once
that April night
    we were on our way to storm the Presidential Palace,
Chema, he was tortured and murdered)
I just tell them: "I met your father"

In the choir loft, slides (radiant colors) of the Debris.
Corita (ex-sister Corita) gave 6 paintings to help Managua.
        Daniel Berrigan is expecting me tomorrow.

Central Park (uptown): And I tell myself: that's where the swans are.
I remember my Liana, and the swans.
She got married. The swans must still be there.
Once, one hungry day, Louis trying to catch a swan.
Once again I saw people talking to themselves in the streets
        "The Lonely Crowd."
With Napoleon and Jackie in Times Square, nothing to see
and along 48th Street among the titillating porn movies.
        An empty store, 2 policemen taking notes
           its window front shattered, and no one looking (right on
           Broadway)

With Daniel Berrigan at the Thomas Merton Center
Daniel (Dan) in blue-jeans and sandals like me, his hair
        "a street kid's hair after a fight"
and the same smile he flashed in the pictures as he was arrested
by the FBI (jubilant between the glum FBI agents)
    he'd read my *Psalms* in prison.
Also there, Jim Forest (a pacifist) with a big mustache
younger than I thought. He wrote me once.
He told me that Merton gave him a crucifix that I made in Gethsemani.
    He's in from Washington, from a protest march
from the Watergate Building to the Justice Department.
And Berrigan sitting on a desk, his lean face propped
on one knee, and his thin hair in his face. Barely recovered
from jail, they tell me. And a girl:
    "The tortures that *aren't supposed* to take place in the United States"
This is a group of contemplatives and resisters, says Berrigan.
    Meeting one night in a Harlem convent
    they got the idea of establishing this Merton Center.
They study the mysticism of different religions
              including the American Indians.
"Merton suffered horrors in the monastery" says Dan

and all of us know it. And Jim reminds us about
when he was forbidden to write against nuclear warfare
because it wasn't a monastic theme.
Dan: "He told me he wouldn't ever become a monk again
but being one already, he'd go on being one."
"He was going to go to Solentiname after Asia, wasn't he?" Jim asks.
        And Dan: "And are you sure he isn't there?"
And Dan also:
"'Contemplation': it's an awful drug we have here.
They meditate. Without thinking at all about the war. Without thinking
at all about the war. You can't be with God and be neutral.
True contemplation is resistance. And poetry,
gazing at the clouds is resistance I found out in jail."
I tell him he ought to go to Cuba. He says he's still on probation.
        I also tell him: "In Latin America
we're integrating Christianity with Marxism."
And he: "I know. But not here.
                Here it's Christianity with Buddhism.
Jim, by now aren't we all Buddhists?
Isn't there any Buddhism in Latin America?"
                                        "No."
Tomorrow, at the Merton Center, they're celebrating
the wedding of his brother, Philip, the other priest,
and ex-nun Elizabeth McAllister—and we're invited.
Philip splashed blood on the draft files in Maryland
then Philip and Daniel burned the files in Catonsville
with home-made napalm (a soap-powder-gasoline mixture)
and Jim also napalmed the files in Milwaukee
        (and they just got out of jail)
They say Merton once considered such an action.
        There's a girl fasting because of the Cambodia bombing.
                On the wall a Berrigan poem about Vietnam
                on big sheets of paper put together like a mural.
When I leave, Dan gives me a fat loaf of bread
a great round loaf of whole-wheat bread, baked there.

To the movies with Napoleon and Jackie for a Cuban film

Memories of Underdevelopment
They don't idealize the Revolution
a documentary segment—a writers congress—
And I believe I saw Roque Dalton in the documentary
Fidel delivering a speech (and part of our audience applauds Fidel).
A crowd of people on the sidewalk arriving in evening clothes: the Opera.
Tony's aristocratic Italian grandfather
left him a villa on the outskirts of Rome.
He's probably going to give it to someone. He doesn't want to own
property.
And Tony said: "Holy Communion . . ." (with burning eyes)
"Communion is my greatest union with people each day. For me,
Communion is the most revolutionary thing in the world"

Philip Berrigan and Elizabeth McAllister
accused by the FBI of plotting to kidnap Kissinger.
Their wedding celebration is at the Merton Center.
Contemplatives and radicals, pacifists, many of them ex-prisoners
Christian Anarchists and Christian Buddhists
and, at this party, a Eucharist with protest songs
sitting on the floor
after the Gospel, Jim and Dan talk, and a young lady
who's just poured blood on Nixon's dining table
and smeared the dining room walls with blood, on a *tourist tour*
of the White House (the press never reported it). She is pregnant,
awaiting trial and maybe years in jail.
Dan Berrigan consecrates a loaf of bread like the one he gave me
and little glasses of wine. The broken bread passes from hand to hand,
and the wine.
Then a collection . . . for the poor Watergate defendants
"enemies and *brothers* of ours."
Back to the party. Dan says: "No more religion."
Gallons of California "white wine" and "rosé" on one table
raisin pudding, apple pie, cheese, on another table.
A very long-haired blond young man, Michael Cullen, greets me.
He used to read my *Psalms* in prison, he says,
and I've read about him.

He hands me a pamphlet he's giving out: *If Mike Cullen Is Deported*
He was born on a farm in the south of Ireland; he came at age 10, not
to make money. He studied at a seminary. Got married, sold insurance
but he was troubled by the rat-infested apartments
        and the blood gushing in Indochina
he burned his draft card. Along with Jim
he burned the draft files in Milwaukee
        the cards marked 1-A to burn bodies in Asia
now they want to deport him, he believes they'll deport him he says sadly
someone passing by stuffs some money in his pocket and tells him
        "keep going" and he smiles (sadly)
he tells me: "The American Dream has become a nightmare."
All the TV cameras on Philip and his wife.
"I believe in the revolution" he says "My contribution is nonviolent"
Blue-eyed Phil. Husky like a football player
                "the Gary Cooper of the Church"
Elizabeth's sweet: she says they've married to help each other in
        the struggle
and they'll create a commune to help others carry on the struggle.
                Dan with his radiant smile
                and his Zen peace

Leaving the Doubleday Bookstore, on 5th Ave
a few men and women in white tunics dancing on the sidewalk
and the young men with shaved heads (in white) look like Trappist
        novices.
                In a shop window:
        Mink. A Persian Lamb Leather Jacket.
        A brooch of diamonds and rubies . . .
A young fellow with a campaign button on his chest: IMPEACH
        NIXON
                Plastic women.
I cross the street in fear: WALK—DON'T WALK (in red)
The clerks in the stores almost all Cubans
and I think I'm hearing talk
by revolutionaries.
The sky filthy. Police sirens.

Old women talking to themselves.
Coronel was telling about that French Dominican here, who told him:
"Since I came 3 months ago I haven't been able to say prayers."
Museum of Modem Art. No time to stop in. And what for?
Frank O'Hara used to work here. He wrote his poetry
            on his lunch hour—sandwiches and Coca Cola.
We once wrote to each other.
Now I've bought his *Lunch Poems* ($1.50) at Brentano's
and the cars remind me of his death
        Run over in New York (on his lunch hour?)
                    WALK—DON'T WALK
Dorothy Day expects me at the *Catholic Worker* says Tony.
On the telephone, she remembered she'd once written to me.

A "paperback" bookstore on 5th Ave.
Many books about the Indians. Pawnee. Sioux. Hopi. The Hopi,
anarchists and pacifists for 2000 years, Gandhians having never
    declared
war or signed a treaty (not even with the U.S.A.)
and now I'm on my way to a noon meeting with Kenneth Arnold
my editor for the English *Homenaje a los Indios Americanos*
Black Elk's autobiography is also here
            Once he came to New York with Buffalo Bill
sky-high houses, lights made from the power of thunder,
he says that here he was like a man who'd never had a vision.
Red Fox also with Buffalo Bill. He loved the Indians, he says,
he defended them in Washington. Time for me to meet Kenneth.
He's in from Baltimore. We plan to meet at the Gotham Book Mart.
I Have Spoken—I've got a copy. With Seattle's speech.
            Seattle, wrapped in his blanket like a toga
    with his famous voice, loud and clear for half a mile,
among the tree stumps in a clearing: "My words are like the stars
that never change. Whatever Seattle says the Great Chief in Washington
can rely on like the return of the sun or the seasons . . ."
            Outside it's raining a rain with no smell
and it's almost lunchtime
        NO SMOKING

"And when the last one of my people has died
and they speak of my tribe like a story from the past . . ."
        whisper of tires on rainy streets
      neon reflections on gleaming wet asphalt
". . . and your children's children think themselves alone
in the field, the store, the shop, they will not be alone.
When the streets of your cities are silent and you
think them empty, they will be filled with the spirits of the dead.
Dead did I say? There is no death. Only a change of world."
I leave with books for more homages to the American Indians
and I head for the Gotham Book Mart—3 blocks away—and there is Kenneth.
He's young, bearded. Also there, silver-haired Miss Steloff,
the famous owner of this bookstore. And I was here once
at a party for Edith Sitwell. Miss Steloff
invited Coronel and me and we brought Mimí Hammer.
And Auden was there, and Tennessee Williams, Marianne Moore, Spender . . .
Kenneth brought the cover for *Homage to the American Indians*
and we go half a block to a Chinese restaurant, and
        the lunch was chow mein but first two ice-cold beers.
This abundance of books about Indians, he says,
goes back a year or two. Indian things have become fashionable.
He also has a poem about Indians, or rather
about Buffalo Bill, his great-great-uncle. Yes, the brother of
        his great-grandfather was
Colonel William Frederick Cody (Buffalo Bill)

Tony comes by for me, and he apologizes for the car.
His fell apart. This luxury car belongs to his dad. (Ashamed)
We're invited to lunch by Brother David's mother
(with Napoleon and Jackie). An apartment in an elegant section
of 5th Ave. She's an Austrian Baroness
but she works as a store clerk. She gave away her money.
A girl has brought me a present: a Watergate Poster
—a mugshot of Nixon labelled WANTED
        Brother David says to me
"What would you say to the abbots about the monasteries in the
        United States?"

I laugh. "Seriously. If the abbots all asked for your advice?"
"They wouldn't take it." "But what would you tell them?"
"That they should become Communists."
A girl: "Why society first
instead of the heart? What's inside comes first!"
I tell her: "We are social beings. Social change is not *outside* us."
       The lunch: yogurt with strawberries
       a loaf of dark bread and another even darker, milk
       blue grapes, red apples, yellow bananas,
       honey, the most delicious honey I've ever tasted in my life.
No liquor at this lunch. I'm the only smoker
       ("The air is polluted enough without inhaling more smoke")
Brother David talks with a small string of rosary beads in his hand.
I ask him: "Can you ever integrate Buddhism with Marxism?"
"Through Christianity. You have integrated
Christianity and Marxism, and we here Christianity and Buddhism."
       Tony leaves us to call on his orphans.

12th Street. Joaquín's apartment was around here. In that house,
       I'm almost sure.
A seller of old books in the Village in love with my shirt
       my cotton peasant shirt from Nicaragua
he asks me who designed it.
       A gold sign: MONEY. (Pawnbroker)
I ask for Charles St. A well-dressed man on a bench: Don't
know, he says. Could I spare a dollar? He hasn't eaten in two days.
       Parra was in Chile.
On every television screen Dean testifying against Nixon.

       Washington Square: Rock in the park
amps crazy electronic music frenzied announcers
thousands of longhairs howling with the band black men blondes
       black women
with the band, barefoot bearded wearing beads or rags
howling with the band, dancing on the grass or
stretched out smoking necking drinking canned beer.
A group of lesbians shouting. Beyond them with a banner,

passive before the Methodist, Bible in hand, preaching to them
with a choir of wooden-faced ladies in robes down to their ankles.
       Crossing the street
two gay men with their tongues are licking
the same cone.

The studio of Armando Morales, the Fuse: in the Bowery
the neighborhood of the beggars and the *Catholic Worker*.
It's a storeroom; Without a bath (you bathe in the sink with a sponge
over an edition of the *Times* to keep the floor dry)
with California wine we recall pre-earthquake Managua
facing the Fuse's canvases which the Gallery is selling for $10,000.
The ashtrays, sardine cans—the kind that open with a key,
the lids rolled halfway back; and piles of those ashtrays.
       He explains to me: the Gallery sets the price, and those
are the "stocks" of a painter. A buyer of "Morales"
invests in him as in General Motors. If there's a rise in the price
(the stocks) they'll invest more in him. And if the selling stops
       The Gallery still couldn't cut prices
even if the Fuse is starving to death—the price cut would create a panic
among the "investors" in Morales' intricate colors and mysterious nudes.
He paints his colors, then covers the whole canvas with black.
Then he *shaves* it, with razor blade, scraping off the black, and
he repaints all the colors over the scraping.
"Now I finally know how to paint," he says, "I can paint anything
    I want. What's hard is to know what to paint."
We remember *Las Cinco Hermanas*, that bar in Managua.
We remember some super-muses that we more or less loved.
And the time we found we were on the police list
      of homosexuals—he for being a painter, and I a poet.
And he remembers that whorehouse "La Hortencia" and I tell him
it wasn't where he says, it was somewhere else. And it's not there
     anymore
because later they built the Church of the Redeemer there
     (the Fuse laughs)
and I was already a priest saying Mass there until my superior

stopped me
for my anti-Somoza preaching (the Fuse laughs even louder) and besides
there isn't even a Redeemer now, it collapsed in the earthquake—
        He can't give pictures for the earthquake benefit
            his painting belongs to the Gallery.
On every television Dean kept on testifying against Nixon.

Laughlin is a door-high man, and
(as I already knew through Merton) brimming with love.
After we're inside he asks his wife about Nicanor's wine.
Where's the wine Nicanor left? He takes out of the refrigerator
the Portuguese white wine, Saint What's-his-name that Nicanor left
the last time he was here. We're holding our glasses, about to drink,
when Laughlin lifts his toward heaven like an Offertory:
"To Tom, I'm sure he'll be enjoying this party
wherever he is!" And I: "He's here." Nicanor Parra's wine
is delicious. "It's a curious thing" says Laughlin "after his death
you saw that each friend of his believed he was Merton's closest friend."
After a pause and a sip of wine: "—And each one really was."
He chats with Napoleon Chow about China and with Jackie about Turkey.
He gives us a few of the latest books from New Directions.
We've quickly signed the contract for my book *En Cuba*.
More wine. Margaret Randall seems to be happy in Cuba—that's great.
He feels very friendly toward her, although he doesn't know her.
Then I mention that Laughlin's a good poet, I've translated him, and he says no
Pound told him he wasn't. He slashed through his poems
with his famous pencil. He told him: "Do something useful" and he
became a publisher. Nobody had a publisher back then, only Hemingway.
He was attending "Ezuversity" in Rapallo. He used to have lunch with Pound.
and his wife at the Albergo Rapales. Then swimming or tennis
and reading Villon, Catullus. Pound was his mentor.
        He tells how Somoza once stole a mine from an uncle of his.
—James Laughlin is the grandson of Laughlin the Steel King—
        "Of course he knew" says Laughlin (meaning Nixon)
Nicanor's wine is gone, so we go to a French restaurant
three blocks away.
"He liked solitude a lot and he liked people a lot.

He loved silence—and conversation, too.
Merton was gregarious, you know, and a perfect monk."

Midnight. Tomorrow's *New York Times* already at a tobacco stand
          NIXON KNEW SAYS DEAN (we buy it)
In the subway an Army poster; boys graduating—
    . . . after graduation it's nice to join the Army . . .
And the dark subway cars now go by wildly painted on the outside:
    The names of boys and girls in many colors
    Alice 95   *Bob 106*   *Charles 195*
and the express trains flash by as if they were covered with flowers
(their names and the streets where they live) "they write them
so someone will recognize them, so as to be real" says Napoleon
        painted with every color spray paint
and there are names even a yard high
        Manuel . . . Julia . . . José . . . (many Puerto Ricans)

Slums "without any beauty except for the clouds"
36 East 1st Street (the Bowery)
I was moved as I saw the tiny sign out front: *Catholic Worker*
a fat man lying on the sidewalk asks me softly for a cigarette
    I was moved as I went into this holy place
she wasn't in, but she soon came along the sidewalk with a few
        other women skinny, hunched, her hair white
she's still beautiful at 75
I kiss the saint's hand and she kisses my face.
Like my grandmother Agustina in the fifties (when she could still
        read and she was a reader of this woman)
This is the famous House of Hospitality founded
by Peter Maurin and Dorothy Day during the Great Depression
where food and shelter are free to all who come
    drunks weirdos drug-users bums and the dying
and it's also a pacifist and anarchist movement:
its goal, a society in which it will be easy to be good.
    Soon the poor would be coming in for their supper.
I was studying at Columbia, and even there we heard
that a saint had died in the beggars' neighborhood.

Peter Maurin, agitator and saint
used to preach in the parks:
                    "Fire your bosses." Or
            "Giving and not taking
            makes people human"
In his one and only suit, rumpled and the wrong size. Without a
        bed of his own
in this place that he founded, not even a corner for his books.
    He used to walk without watching the traffic lights.
And she's been devoted since then to
"the works of mercy and rebellion." A life
of daily communion and of taking part
in every strike, demonstration, protest march, or boycott.
They come here to work without wages, students, seminarians,
teachers, sailors, beggars too, and sometimes they stay
all their lives. Many have been in jail or are still there.
Hennacy used to fast in front of the government buildings
with a placard, handing out flyers and selling the paper
and he didn't pay taxes because 85% is for the war
he worked as a farmhand to avoid paying taxes.
Hugh was skinny, in shorts sandals and a poncho, and
        he also did penance in the streets.
Jack English, a brilliant journalist from Cleveland
was the cook for the *Catholic Worker* and later became a monk.
Roger La Porte was a handsome blond 22 years old; he killed himself
by setting himself on fire with gasoline in front of the United Nations.
And an old ex-marine, Smoky Joe, who fought against Sandino
in Nicaragua, died here, a convert to nonviolence.
        Merton worked here before he became a Trappist monk.
The paper still sells for a cent
as it did when Dorothy Day went out to sell it for the first time
        in Union Square one May Day (1933)
It was the third year of the Depression
            12 million unemployed
and Peter wanted the tabloid to be (more than a publication of opinions)
a revolution.
        The pots now steaming

They're beginning to come, the poor, the homeless, the Bowery bums,
to line up. "The other United States" says Dorothy
       men replaced by machines
       and abandoned by Holy Mother State.
Shouts. Someone has bust in kicking and reeling.
Two *Catholic Worker* people gently take him out.
"We *never* call the police because we believe in nonviolence"
And she also tells me: "When I visited Cuba
I saw that Sandino was one of their heroes
and I was glad. Because as a young woman I collected money for him,
when I was a Communist, before my conversion to Catholicism.
And I saw Sandino's top generals (not him)
in Mexico: with their big sombreros, eating hot dogs
      why hot dogs I don't know"
And lively, raising her white head of hair: "I know Castro's Cuba,
as I told you in my letter. I liked it"
Shouts. Now it's a dwarf. And someone gently carries her away
    lifted in the air like a doll.
She says that now they're helping Chavez's workers by
boycotting the A & P chain. And she prays, she says,
for the United States to have a purifying defeat. She talks
about Joan Baez who used to sing in Hanoi during the bombings.
    She says
Hennacy used to say: "Contrary to what people think
it's not us anarchists that are bomb crazy; it's the government."
    And there isn't peace because the streets would be left with
       no traffic
the factories at a standstill, birds singing on top of the machines
as she saw during the Great Depression. She talks about the horrors
she has seen in the Women's House of Detention
the times that she's been in jail. And watching the poor come in
she repeats what Peter used to say: "The future will be different
   if we make the present different"
A reverent good-bye to this anarchist saint
and to this holy place where everyone is welcome, everything free
      to each according to his needs
      from each according to his abilities.

DOWNTOWN. UPTOWN. Bang. Bang. Trains thundering along
underground Uptown and Downtown
with the names of poor children painted like flowers
   Tom   Jim   John   Carolina
their names and the sad addresses where they live. They're
real. So we'll know that they're REAL. Bang bang
the express trains on high tension cables,
their shining ads for Calvert, Pall Mall, and the Army
    it's nice to join the Army

At night, near Wall Street, in an apartment with no furniture
Marxist priests and laymen and Protestant ministers
 "To change the system in which profit is the goal of mankind"
"There is no room for Christian ethics within the limits of private
  morality"
    "The vision of the Kingdom of God is subversive"
One of them works with computers, another with the poor.
Sunday night, and whole floors still lit up on Wall Street.
They're screwing us.
   Hello Bogotá
      Hello ITT
2 twin skyscrapers taller than the Empire State
the whole top half lit up
imperialism looming up in the sky behind the windowpanes
Hello we wanted more drought
 Who is that other monster rising up in the night?
The Chase Manhattan Bank screwing half of humanity.
Behind Wall Street, the Brooklyn Bridge, like a lyre of lights.
In the dark two kids look like they're stripping a car.
  Our pale satellite above the Brooklyn sky
   like a flattened soccer ball.

Early the next day Tony took me back to Kennedy Airport
in his Franciscan car. 6 days in New York.
   The Benefit would be for Conscientization.
"Not for any institution!" Tony told me. *Not for any institution.*
I didn't get a window seat. As we took off, out in the distance

(just a glimpse)
the silhouette of skyscrapers against a sky filled with car exhaust
acids and carbon monoxide.

[J. C.]

We get off the plane and we go, Nicaraguans and foreigners,
all mixed together toward the huge lighted building—first stop
Immigration and Customs—and as we approach, passport in hand,
I think of how proud I am to be holding
the passport of my socialist country, and of my satisfaction
at arriving in a Socialist Nicaragua. "Comrade"
they'll say to me—a revolutionary comrade welcomed
by the revolutionary comrades of Immigration and Customs—
not that there won't be controls; there must be controls
so that capitalism and Somozaism never come back—
and the emotion of coming back to my country during a revolution
with more changes, more and more decrees
of expropriation that I'd hear of, changes more and more radical,
many surprises in the short time I've been away
and I see joy in the eyes of everybody—the ones that have stayed,
the others are gone already—and now we go into the brightness
and they ask natives and foreigners for their passports . . .
but it was all a dream and I am in Somoza's Nicaragua
and they take away my passport with the icy courtesy
with which Security would tell me "Please come in"
and they take the passport inside and they don't bring it back (surely
they must surely be phoning Security
or the Presidential Palace or somebody or other) and by now
all the other passengers are gone and I don't know if I'll be arrested
but no: at the end of an hour they come back with my passport.
The CIA must have known that this time I didn't go to Cuba
and that I was just a single day in East Berlin,
and so at last I can go through Customs
all alone in Customs with my ancient suitcase
and the kid that inspects just pretends to inspect
without inspecting anything and he murmurs to me: "Father"
and he doesn't dig deep down into the suitcase where he would find
the phonograph record with Allende's last appeal to the people
from the Palace, interrupted by the sound of bombs exploding,
the record I bought in East Berlin, or Fidel's speech
about Allende's overthrow, the one Sergio gave me,
and the kid says: "It's eight o'clock already and we haven't had supper,

us Customs workers get hungry, too."
"What time do you have your supper?" I ask "Not till after the last plane lands"
and now I'm moving toward the dark demolished city
where everything is just the same and nothing's going on but I have seen
his eyes and with his eyes he has said to me: "Comrade."

[D. D. W.]

That top-secret flight at night.
We might have been shot down. The night calm and clear.
The sky teeming, swarming with stars. The Milky Way
so bright behind the thick pane of the plane window,
    a sparkling white mass in the black night
with its millions of evolutionary and revolutionary changes.
We were going over the water to avoid Somoza's air force,
        but close to the coast.
The small plane flying low, and flying slow.
First the lights of Rivas, taken and retaken by Sandinistas,
    now almost in Sandinista hands.
Then other lights: Granada, in the hands of the Guard
                      (it would be attacked that night).
Masaya, completely liberated. So many fell there.
Farther out a bright glow: Managua. Site of so many battles.
(The Bunker.) Still the stronghold of the Guard.
Diriamba, liberated. Jinotepe, fighting it out. So much heroism
glitters in those lights. Montelimar—the pilot shows us:
the tyrant's estate near the sea. Puerto Somoza, next to it.
The Milky Way above, and the lights of Nicaragua's revolution.
Out there, in the north, I think I see Sandino's campfire.
            ("That light is Sandino.")
The stars above us, and the smallness of this land
but also its importance, these
tiny lights of people. I think: everything is light.
The planet comes from the sun. It is light turned solid.
This plane's electricity is light. Its metal is light. The warmth of life
    comes from the sun.
        "Let there be light."
There's darkness too.
There are strange reflections—I don't know where they're from—
    on the clear surface of the windows.
A red glow: the taillights of the plane.
And reflections on the calm sea: they must be stars.
I look at the light from my cigarette—it also comes from the sun,
    from a star.
And the outline of a great ship. The U.S. aircraft carrier

sent to patrol the Pacific coast?
A big light on our right startles us. A jet attacking?
No. The moon coming out, a half-moon, so peaceful, lit by the sun.
    The danger of flying on such a clear night.
And suddenly the radio. Jumbled words filling the small plane.
The Guard? The pilot says: "It's our side."
            They're on our wavelength.
Now we're close to León, the territory liberated.
A burning reddish-orange light, like the red-hot tip of a cigar: Corinto:
the powerful lights of the docks flickering on the sea.
And now at last the beach at Poneloya, and the plane coming in to land,
the string of foam along the coast gleaming in the moonlight.
    The plane coming down. A smell of insecticide.
And Sergio tells me: "The smell of Nicaragua!"
It's the most dangerous moment, enemy aircraft
                may be waiting for us over this airport.
And the airport lights at last.
We've landed. From out of the dark come olive-green-clad comrades
to greet us with hugs.
We feel their warm bodies—that also come from the sun,
that also are light.
            This revolution is fighting the darkness.
It was daybreak on July 18th. And the beginning
    of all that was about to come.

                                                        [J. C.]

VISION FROM THE BLUE PLANE-WINDOW

In the round little window, everything is blue,
land bluish, blue-green, blue
                          (and sky)
          everything is blue
blue lake and lagoons
                    blue volcanoes
while farther off the land looks bluer
        blue islands in a blue lake.
This is the face of the land liberated.
And where all the people fought, I think:
                              for love!
To live without the hatred
                    of exploitation.
To love one another in a beautiful land
so beautiful, not only in itself
              but because of the people in it,
above all because of the people in it.
That's why God gave us this beautiful land
for the society in it.
And in all those blue places they fought, suffered
          for a society of love
                    here in this land.

One patch of blue looks more intense . . .
And I thought I was seeing the sites of all the battles there,
and of all the deaths,
behind that small, round windowpane
                        blue
                all the shades of blue.

In September more coyotes were seen near San Ubaldo.
More alligators, soon after the victory,
    in the rivers, out by San Ubaldo.
        Along the highway more rabbits, weasels . . .
The bird population has tripled, we're told,
    especially tree ducks.
The noisy tree ducks fly down to swim
            where they see the water shining.

Somoza's people also destroyed the lakes, rivers, and mountains.
    They altered the course of the rivers for their farms.
The Ochomogo dried up last summer.
The Sinecapa dried up because the big landowners stripped the land.
The Rio Grande in Matagalpa, all dried up, during the war,
      out by the Sébaco Plains.
They put two dams in the Ochomogo,
          and the capitalist chemical wastes
spilled into the Ochomogo and the fish swam around as if drunk.
      The Boaco River filled with sewage.
The Moyuá Lagoon dried up. A Somocist colonel
robbed the lands from peasants, and built a dam.
The Moyuá Lagoon that for centuries had been so beautiful.
(But the little fish will soon return.)
They stripped the land and they dammed the rivers.
    Hardly any iguanas sunning themselves,
             hardly any armadillos.
Somoza used to sell the green turtle of the Caribbean.
They exported turtle eggs and iguanas by the truckload.
     The loggerhead turtle being wiped out.
José Somoza was wiping out the sawfish of the Great Lake.
In danger of extinction the jungle's tiger cat,
    its soft, jungle-colored fur,
and the puma, the tapir in the mountains
(like the peasants in the mountains).
And poor Rio Chiquito! Its misfortune
the whole country's. Somocism mirrored in its waters.
The Rio Chiquito in León, fed by streams

of sewage, wastes from soap factories and tanneries,
white water from soap factories, and red from tanneries;
plastics on the bottom, chamber pots, rusty iron. Somocism
left us that.
(We will see it clear and pretty again singing toward the sea.)
And into Lake Managua all of Managua's sewage water
and chemical wastes.
And out by Solentiname, on the island La Zanata:
a great stinking white heap of sawfish skeletons.

But the sawfish and the freshwater shark could finally breathe again.
Tisma is teeming once more with herons
                              reflected in its mirrors.
It has many grackles, tree ducks, kingfishers, teals.
            The plant life has benefited as well.
The armadillos go around very happy with this government.
            We will save the woodlands, rivers, lagoons.
We're going to decontaminate Lake Managua.
The humans weren't the only ones who longed for liberation.
The whole ecology had been moaning. The Revolution
also belongs to lakes, rivers, trees, animals.

[J. C.]

THE PARROTS

My friend Michel is a commanding officer in Somoto,
        near the border with Honduras,
and he told me about finding a shipment of parrots
that were going to be smuggled to the United States
        in order for them to learn to speak English.
There were 186 parrots, and 47 had already died in their cages.
And he took them back to the place from where they'd been taken,
and when the truck was getting close to a place called The Plains
near the mountains where those parrots came from
        (the mountains looked immense behind those plains)
the parrots began to get excited and beat their wings
        and press themselves against the walls of their cages.
And when the cages were opened
they all flew like arrows in the same direction to their mountains.
That's just what the Revolution did with us, I think:
it freed us from cages
        in which we were being carried off to speak English.
It brought us back to the Homeland from which we'd been uprooted.

Comrades in fatigues green as parrots
        gave the parrots their green mountains.
        But there were 47 dead.

[J. C.]

VISIT TO WEIMAR (GDR)

We were passing through Weimar and naturally
                    we went to Goethe's house.
His paintings were there. A Lucas Cranach . . .
      An Italian primitive . . .
Also a delicate pencil drawing he made
      of his pretty wife asleep in the garden.
The piano where the young Mendelssohn played.
Greek statues, his collection of minerals.
      The desk where he wrote *Faust*.
His poor bed. The armchair where he died.
Very elegant drawing rooms because he was Prime Minister; his bedroom
      modest like Lenin's in the Kremlin.
The couch where he used to spend all night talking
                with the Prince of Weimar.
"Profound thoughts concerning nature and art."
A time he devoted more to the natural sciences than to poetry.
Here he discovered the intermaxillary bone in man.
Also the vertebrae theory of the skull.
In 1790 he began the study which led to his theory of colors.
(The same year that he wrote *The Metamorphosis of Plants*.)
It was a snowy day when Schiller came to Weimar to live.
      He had a conversation with Napoleon here.
        In 1815 he was appointed Prime Minister.
      (He was also a kind of Minister of Culture.)
This was the intellectual capital of Germany.
      Here young Heine, boasting, told him
      that he too was at work writing "his" Faust.
      And that the plums in Weimar were so delicious!
      The devastating effect that Schiller's death had on him.
The Botanical Garden in Palermo revealed the proto-plant to him.
Working on *The Metamorphosis of Animals*
he became more and more convinced
that the art of poetry is "a common property of mankind"
and in all times and places it exists in thousands of people.
      Poetry writing could be taught to the masses.
All that mattered to him were culture and barbarism, he said.
      He was ending up alone.

In 1827 his Charlotte died:
            The next year, the Grand Duke.
But he had written: "There is always a quiet in the treetops."
At the end of Book II, Faust, now blind, has the vision
of "a free people living on this earth."
He put a lock on the covers of Book II
and stuck it in a cabinet he locked so that no one could read it.
Later on, he no longer left his room to go into the elegant drawing rooms.
The day he was dying in his armchair
        he thought he saw a letter from Schiller on the floor.
And 15 minutes from there
                forests all around
We enter the "Highway of Blood."
        The prisoners themselves paved it.
 It ends at deserted platforms.
        where hundreds and hundreds and hundreds of trains used to come.
The imposing bronze doors open for us,
                 with a flowered grille
and big letters backwards, above the grille,
that only can be read inside, once the doors have closed:
EVERYONE RECEIVES WHAT HE DESERVES
like the entrance to Dante's Inferno
    Lasciate ogni speranza, o voi che entrate
       It's the entrance to Buchenwald.
Barbed-wire fences inside of barbed-wire fences inside
             of other electrified barbed-wire fences.
       The horrifying turrets.
And we saw the red-brick ovens of the crematorium.
The "special" cells of the ones who resisted,
where before dying heroes cried out
             from the little hole with bars,
to the whole camp, not to surrender.
It was truly another town.
       With as many inhabitants as Weimar.
Their bodies walking skeletons
     a tottering footstep
         a blank stare full of terror.

Everything well planned.
The name of each person who was going to arrive
announced beforehand at the concentration camp
with a copy to the Central Office of Concentration Camps,
cc: Gestapo, etc.
>   "In reference to what has previously been
>   discussed I enclose in duplicate, for the
>   necessary purposes, the list of those unable to
>   do work"
>   *(Signed)*
>   Camp Doctor of Buchenwald.
On the outskirts, mounds of corpses.
The grey building with different floors where they left their clothes.
Girls wearing elegant dresses
        came out wearing the blue-and-white striped uniform
with a number tattooed on their left arm
            many soon dying of sheer grief.
Human skin was good for parchment.
    For writing poems on it, romantic ones.
    For binding books.
        For lampshades.
They shrunk Jewish heads (like the Jívaros), for souvenirs.
And doctors doing all kinds of experiments on live bodies.
There were 18-hour workdays in December, out in the snow and wind,
        wearing just a thin jacket,
and many were so cold they threw themselves on the
                            barbed-wire to be electrocuted.
The children put in a separate pen
their barbed-wire pen inside of barbed-wire fences
                        inside of more barbed-wires.
Next to them a small barbed-wire cage with bear cubs
        (the children loving those cubs)
and when the children cried from hunger
the guards poured plenty of milk for the bear cubs
        so that the children might see it,
                            the cute little bears
and the children crying, screaming.

Floodlights revolving in the fog, revolving,
      searching for a fugitive
and the gruff barking of the police dogs behind the barbed-wire fences
        and its echoes.
One could tell if they were burning corpses in the ovens
if the smoke coming out was black or white.
    And from the delicious smell of roasting meat.
The voice of the pastor admonishing them, gripping the bars
      in the final cell.
We saw the apparatus "for measuring a prisoner's height"
and the little window behind it that opened up and out
                       came a hand with a pistol
    to shoot him in the back of the neck.
Before, a "doctor" examined his teeth
      looking for gold.
The fact is they'd discovered the dead bodies yielded money;
Hair, gold teeth, fat, skin for artwork.
      Capitalist economy to the point of madness.
   "Contents of shipment:
      2 kilos of hair in locks and braids"
The death trains always pulling up to the platforms.
And in Weimar nobody knew anything.
They only saw a forbidden zone and a long line of trains.
But they got suspicious
when an army truck crashed right in the center of town
and piles of corpses fell onto the street.
      These were the forests where Goethe would go for walks.
Close to here the oak tree that Goethe used to read beneath.
   And that the Nazis took good care of.

[J. C.]

AMONG FACADES

We're going through the streets of a neighborhood in New York,
small shops, a restaurant, *Dry Cleaning*,
apartment houses, three-, four-stories high,
made of red brick, concrete, grey brick,
    then we pass through a hamlet in the Alps,
   cobblestone streets in a Mexican village,
then a river with a medieval mill,
    a dusty street in a town in the West,
   with its saloons, a window with broken glass,
on a hill an 11th-century castle,
and once again apartment houses, a bank, liquor stores
   in any city in the United States,
but if you knock on anything, it sounds hollow,
    everything is plasterwork,
   they're only the outside walls, there's nothing in back.
A policeman in the middle of the street, with his badge
    and book for giving out tickets,
might be a real policeman or a famous actor.
And the producer (Ed Lewis) who is showing me everything tells me:
"no director, no producer, nobody
    runs the show in a movie,
   just the bank putting up the money."
And on leaving and seeing the bank, restaurants, *Dry Cleaning*,
I thought whatever I'd knock on would sound hollow,
Hollywood, all of Los Angeles, everything
   was merely walls
    with nothing in back.

[J. C.]

They had a happy childhood on the banks of the Hudson
on a 3500-acre estate
     with 11 mansions and 8 swimming pools
    and 1500 servants
      and a great house of toys
but when they grew up they moved into Room 5600
(actually the 55th and 56th floors of the tallest skyscraper
at Rockefeller Center)
where hundreds and hundreds of foundations and corporations
are managed like
      —what truly is—
    a single *fortune.*
Dependent on Room 5600 the millionaires in Venezuela
private enterprise in Brazil
    and you and I.
First there were ads in newspapers and on radios
         in Latin America
coming from that Room 5600
     ("a formative education for the young Rockefellers
in the vulnerabilities of the press")
all the programs involving the press divided into 2 categories
    "economic warfare" and "psychological warfare"
using news to make, explained Nelson to the Senate,
the same thing the military makes.
And Room 5600 used to have secret "observers"
     (kind of the first offspring of the present CIA)
providing information about owners, editorial politics,
personal opinions . . . even the least little reporter,
from which came their "propaganda analysis," dossiers
systematically organized on Latin American public opinion.
So in Room 5600
they learned the basics
of handling the news.
"They soon discovered that *news*
doesn't stem from facts
but from interest groups." And so that was how
the news about Latin America (edited in Washington)

with economic incentives and economic pressures
reached Latin America from Room 5600
together with slick editorials, telephotos, flashes, "exclusive"
feature stories
            (and Walt Disney for the movies)
until 80% of the world news for Latin America
(originating in Washington)
was tightly controlled and monitored in New York
by Room 5600,
and so all the businesses in Latin America
(and its misery)
                are linked to that Room 5600.
An operation that just required enough money
from Room 5600.
                Our minds, our passions.
The thoughts of the lady who runs a boardinghouse.
                The man walking some lonely beach.
A silhouette of lovers kissing in the moonlight
(influenced more by Room 5600 than by the moon)
Whatever Octavio Paz or Pablo Antonio Cuadra thinks.
Whether you say rose or say Russia
Room 5600 influences that.
Our perceptions conditioned by Room 5600.
And thousands of Latin American journalists
invited by Room 5600
to Miami Beach where everything is fake, even the sea is fake,
a servile sea in front of your hotel.
And so
        NICARAGUA A TOTALITARIAN COUNTRY
THE SANDINISTAS ARE PERSECUTING THE CHURCH
                MISKITOS MASSACRED
TERRORISTS . . .
That's why, American journalists, La Prensa is censored.
        Monopoly of what the public reads, hears, sees
as they fill the air with carbon monoxide, mercury, lead.
As for the press:
            "Silence was imposed on the poor"

Thanks to Nelson. To David, the younger one,
Chase Manhattan Bank
—"tied to almost every important business in the world"—
right in Room 5600
where the whole huge and scattered fortune
is only one fortune, there in one single Office.
With as many public-relations people in Room 5600
as they had servants in their childhood.
So their image changed from criminals to philanthropists.
            About whom, it is said, they did
everything, as with oil, with American politics,
except refining it.
            Corporations growing like a carcinoma.
And because of Room 5600
the holy family set up in garbage dumps.
Children playing by streams loaded with shit
                because of their monopolies.
Their monopolies that are getting fat on malnutrition.
Monopolies raising the price of the planet,
                bread and wine,
joys, medicines, *The Divine Comedy.*
Manhattan from offshore looking like a sacred mountain
and the seemingly heavenly skyscrapers raised
                                by the profiteering
in one of them:
                Room 5600, its lights Luciferian.
The shining waters of Lake Erie without fish
because of its sewers, the ones from Room 5600.
                        Ducks drenched with oil.
Poison wind over deserts and dead rivers.
Contaminating the species with radioactive iodine
                                Room 5600.
Manufacturing chocolates or napalm, it's the same to them.
And they manufacture *facts.*
At dusk you see from your car, above sulfurous bogs
the flickering fires of the oil refineries like Purgatory
and above them like a city in Oz

the glass skyscrapers lit up
        Wall Street and Rockefeller Center
with its Room 5600.
Every secretary of state since Dean Acheson
        that is, ever since I was 25 years old
has worked for a Rockefeller organization.
                "Do you remember those new companies
                    coveted on the Stock Exchange like nubile girls?"
Their orgies with voluptuous and smiling bonuses
in Room 5600.
                "Does Rembrandt pay dividends?"
And the dividends from the Vietnam War.
        The profits from ESSO high as the stratosphere.
1 gallon of gas that cost the planet to produce it
1 million dollars . . .
        And Venezuela sold its oil for trinkets.
        Twelve-year-old girls up for sale in the Northeast.
                        The cassava bread sour.
            Sterilization of women in the Amazon.
Monopoly even of life itself.
The millions flowing to them as if in pipelines
        owners of lands banks industries human beings
as if in pipelines from where the oilfields are huge
and the leases dirt-cheap.
They flooded New York with "moral bonds"
            (that is, phony bonds)
Hence New York's bankruptcy
due to the billions in "moral bonds" from Room 5600.
Terrifying nations with cruel stories.
Its bat-like shadow over the culture, the academies.
                All the weight of the presses on us.
Subjected to the whims of their stock companies.
That's why, Daniel Berrigan, Nicaragua's boys are fighting.
            Whether milk or poison
                    the product doesn't matter
            bread or napalm
                    the product doesn't matter.

David for instance had lunch with a Mr. Carter on Wall Street
and after lunch
    he picked him to be President of the United States.
They continued their happy childhood
in Room 5600.

AT THE GRAVE OF A GUERRILLA

I think about your body that's been decomposing underground
turning into soft earth, humus once more
together with the humus of all the other humans
who have existed and will exist on our little globe
making all of us together fertile earth of our planet Earth.
And when the cosmonauts look at this blue and pink ball
                                        in the black night
what they will be seeing, far off, is your shining tomb
            (your tomb and the tomb of us all)
and when the beings from somewhere in outer space
            look at this dot of Earth's light
they will be seeing your tomb.
And one day it will all be a tomb, one silent tomb,
and there will no longer be any living beings on the planet, comrade.
        And then?
Then we will decompose more, we will fly, atoms in the cosmos.
And perhaps matter is eternal, brother,
without beginning or end or it has an end and begins again each time.
Your love surely had a beginning but it has no end.
And your atoms that were in the soil of Nicaragua,
your loving atoms, that sacrificed themselves for love,
you'll see, they will turn into light,
I imagine your particles in the vastness of the cosmos like banners
like living posters.
                I don't know if I'm making myself clear.
What I do know is that your name will never be forgotten
and forever will be shouted: Present!

[J. C.]

PLURIVERSE, 1986–2005

In the beginning
        —before space-time—
   was the Word
All that is, then, is true.
           Poem.
Things exist in the form of word.
All was night, &c.
   There was no sun, nor moon, nor people, nor animals, nor plants.
The word was. (Amorous word.)
Mystery and at the same time expression of that mystery.
What is and at the same time expresses what it is.
"When in the beginning there was not yet anyone
         he created the words (*naikino*)
and gave them to us, just like the yucca"
in that anonymous yellowing translation from the German
of a part of that massive book by Presuss
which I came across in Bogotá's Museum of Ethnography
  a Spanish translation of Presuss translating from Witoto into German:
   The word in their songs, which he gave them, they say,
is the same with which he made the rain
    (he made it rain with his word & a drum),
the dead go to a region where "they speak words well"
downriver: the river is very big,
   (what they've heard of the Amazon according to Presuss)
there they haven't died again
    & they are well downriver without dying.
The day will come when we will head downriver ourselves.
In the beginning, then, was the word.
The one that is & communicates what it is.
      That is:
the one that totally expresses itself.
   Secret that surrenders itself. A yes.
 He in himself is a yes.
Reality revealed.
   Eternal reality which eternally reveals itself.
At the beginning . . .
      Before space-time,

before there was before,
at the beginning, when there wasn't even beginning,
at the beginning,
                was the reality of the word.
When all was night, when
all beings were still obscure, before being beings,
a voice existed, a clear word,
                a song in the night.

In the beginning was the Song.
        Singing he created the cosmos.
And for that reason all things sing.
They don't dance except through words (through which the world was created)
say the Witotos. "We do not dance without a reason."
And the huge trees of the forest were born,
the canaguche palm, with its fruit for us to drink,
likewise the choruco-monkey to eat the trees,
the tapir that eats the fruit on the ground,
the small parrot, the borugo to eat the jungle,
he created all the animals like the otter, that eats fish,
and the small otter,
he made all the animals like the stag & the chonta-stag,
in the air the royal eagle that eats the chorucos,
he created the sidyi, the picon, the kuyudo parakeet,
the eifoke and forebeke turkey, the chilanga, the hokomaike,
the patilico, the sarok parakeet,
the kuikudyo, the fuikango, the siva & the tudyagi,
the stinking duck, the mariana that now knows how to eat fish,
the dyivuise, the siada, the hirina & the himegisinyos
and the Witoto poem goes on
in the anonymous Spanish translation
from Presuss's German translation of the Witoto
        filed away in the Museum.
    "Although they say: they dance for no reason. We
    in our festivities tell the tales."
Which Presuss patiently gathered on a gramophone years ago
and translated into German.

The dead: they have returned to the creative word
whence they sprang with the rain, the fruit & the songs.
 "If our traditions were merely absurd,
  we would be sad in our feasts."
    And the rain a word from his mouth.
He created the world by means of a dream.
And he himself is something like a dream. A dream that dreams.
They call him *Naineuma*, according to Presuss:
      "The one who is (or has) something non-existent."
Or like a dream that became real without losing its dream mystery.
Naineuma: "The one who is SOMETHING very real non-existent."
And the earth is *Nicarani*, "that dreamed," or "the vision dreamed":
that born from nothing like a dream of the Father.
Genesis according to the Witoto or Huitoto or Uitoto.
In the beginning
        before the Big Bang
            was the Word.
There was no light
light was within the darkness
and he brought the light out of the darkness
drew the two apart
and that was the Big Bang
or the first Revolution.
      Word that never passes
          ("heaven & earth will pass away . . .")
A distant murmur from that explosion
lingers on in the universe
        like radio static.
          And the celestial dialectical dance began.
"The *yang* calls;
  the *yin* responds."
      He is in that which each thing is.
            And in that which each thing enjoys.
        Each thing coitus.
          The entire cosmos copulation.
All things love, and he is the love with which they love.
"The *yang* calls;

the *yin* responds."
They are the two choruses.
They are the two choruses which take turns singing.
And Pythagoras discovered the harmony of the universe
    hearing a blacksmith hammer.
That is: the isotropic movement—uniform and harmonious—
                      of the universe.
Creation is a poem.
    Poem, which is "creation" in Greek and thus
St. Paul calls God's Creation, POIEMA,
like a poem by Homer Padre Ángel used to say.
Each thing is like a "like."
    Like a "like" in a Huidobro poem.
The entire cosmos copulation.
    And each thing is word,
           word of love.
    Only love reveals
        but it veils what it reveals,
alone it reveals,
    alone lover & beloved
in the illuminated solitude,
        the nights of the lovers,
word that never passes
        while the water flows beneath the bridge
        & the slow moon above the houses passes.
The cosmos
      secret word in the nuptial chamber.
        Each thing that is is verbal.
Lie is what is not.
           And each thing is secret.
Listen to the murmur of things . . .
    They say it, but say it in secret.
Only alone is it revealed.
    Only at night in a secret place does it lay itself bare.
      The cosmic blushing.
Nature: timid, bashful.
    All things lower their eyes in your presence.

    —My secret is for my beloved alone.
And space is not speechless.
   Who has ears to hear let him hear.
     We are surrounded by sound.
Everything existing united by rhythm.
   Cosmic jazz not chaotic or cacophonous.
In harmony. He made all things singing and the cosmos sings.
    Cosmos like a dark record that spins & sings
     in the dead of night
or romantic radio borne to us on the wind.
Each thing sings.
   Things, not created by calculus
      but by poetry.
By the Poet ("Creator" = POIÊTÊS)
Creator of the POIEMA.
   With finite words an infinite meaning.
Things are words to whoever understands them.
    As though all were telephone or radio or t.v.
   Words in an ear.
Do you hear those frogs?
    & do you know what they wish to tell us?
Do you hear those stars? They have something to tell us.
    The chorus of things.
Secret melody of the night.
Aeolian harp that sounds alone at the mere brush of the air.
   The cosmos sings.
     The two choruses.
"The *yang* calls;
 the *yin* responds."
     Dialectically.
Do you hear those stars? It is love that sings.
   The silent music.
    The sonorous solitude.
"The music in silence of the moon," said mad Cortés.
Matter is waves.
    And waves? Questions.
An I towards a you.

That is searching for a you.
And this because each being is word.
Because the word made the world
we can communicate in the world.
—His word and a drum . . .
We are word
in a world born of the word
and which exists only as something spoken.
A secret of two lovers in the night.
The firmament announces it as with neon letters.
Each night swapping secrets with another night.
People are words.
And thus one is not if one is not dialogue.
And so then each one is two
or is not.
Each person is for another person.
I am not I rather you are I!
One is the I of a you
or one is nothing.
I am nothing more than you otherwise if not I am not!
I am yes. I am Yes to a you, to a you for me,
to a you for me.
People are dialogue, I say,
if not their words would touch nothing
like waves in the cosmos picked up by no radio,
like messages to uninhabited planets,
or a bellowing in the lunar void
or a telephone call to an empty house.
(A person alone does not exist.)
I tell you again, my love:
I am you and you are me.
I am: love.

[J. L.]

Our cycle follows the star cycle:
stars are born, grow, die; our cycle is short
     —theirs too.
They seem stable
but like us they're slowly dying.
The second law of thermodynamics maintains
that a star is a passing phenomenon.
The black hole in which we are and call universe . . .
The second law of thermodynamics predicts
there can only be one end to the universe:
to die of cold.
And scientists say: it will go on expanding forever,
and the distance between particle and particle will be greater
than the diameter of the observable universe today.
     All process finished.
              The universe stabilized.

     The final state of matter.
         That's entropy.
And something that increases over time.
An irreversible progression towards disorder,
until total disorder of matter is reached.
Entropy is time that runs away
and never returns.
The exponential curves of their bodies:
all the girls I loved—
entropy took them away.

Where a star once was
only blackness and emptiness remain,
     a black hole.
The Second Law:
that things may be more but never less chaotic.
Thermodynamic equilibrium when all change ceases . . .
The stars' disequilibrium won't last forever.
Joyful disequilibrium, their burning in the cold spaces.
         And where there's nothing left anymore, merely

solitary black holes.
Black hole after black hole after black hole
from which neither light nor astronauts
will ever again return.

Our lives elapse at the speed of light
which is Relativity's only absolute,
of light that never slows down nor ever turns back.
            Never turns back. Sad astrophysics.
Sad astrophysics of the lonely lover in the night.

Those who are in the Centaur
see the sun in Cassiopeia
simply as one more star.
They know nothing of us.
You and I in Cassiopeia . . . while
those in the Centaur know nothing of Earth's death.

                Space is without substance
                and it's its nothingness which is curved.
And Wheeler:
"There's nothing in the world except empty curved space."
            Where reality is like a dream.
            Undulations of nothingness.
            Atoms in their confused world of semi-existence.
Reality turned out to be waves
but not like the waves that break on a rock
nor sound nor light waves,
but elusive voluble waves of probabilities.
And our bodies are made from them,
solid bodies with life insurance policies,
identity documents, halted at traffic lights,
enclosed in offices, with Newtonian routines.
And at night above us the questioning stars
they too waves of probability like us,
never having a reality like us
were it not for an observer like us who

undulate in waves of probability.
      With creation the expansion began.
            And blue stars in the distance shiver . . .
They say that since an infinity of worlds exists
there's a world in which Napoleon won at Waterloo.
And a world in which she accepted my love in Granada.
But those worlds and ours will never come together.

Quantic waves are oscillations of possibility.
Quantic waves which have been called empty waves.
But in quantum theory no "nothing" exists.
Also an electron "has literally no dimension."
Or:
      "it's not an object as we understand it."
(An electron.)
Particles are no more solid nor more permanent,
they say, than the shapes of the gush of a fountain.
To Heisenberg, no more substantial than a promise.
It's thought that if space-time were seen
it would have the form of foam.
Bertrand Russell couldn't answer the taxi driver.
Very old, he climbed into a taxi and the driver recognized him,
and asked: "What's it all about then?"
For the first time in his life he couldn't answer.

If the universe is expanding
from which center is it expanding?
Or is every point the center?
So then the center of the universe
is also our galaxy,
is also our planet
(and the girl who once was for me).

To have a rational description of the universe!
"The fact that it is *universe* and not *diverse*."
      A space so immense
      for the immensity of time.

Space and time that cannot be separated:
to talk of space is time and vice versa.
It has never been proved in an experiment that time passes.
That we pass is another matter. Myriam, Adelita.
Atomic movements are reversible,
but we, composed of atoms,
alas, we are not reversible.
The film does not run backwards.
                    That's entropy.
Anaxagoras believed the sun to be the size of Peloponnesia.
That not so far back. Now so many galaxies
have been seen like a uniform gas of galaxies.
One hundred solar systems are born every second
in the explorable universe,
according to Sagan.
And in many perhaps a third planet
with beaches and palm trees and women
and with some Sagan,
and a lonely poet singing to the stars.
                    Entropy took them away.

On a scale in which the galaxies are dust particles . . .
The center everywhere and nowhere.
But if the oldest galaxies are accelerating
we are slowing down.
                    What can there be beyond the furthest reaches?
                    The edge of the universe?
Out there where the galaxies appear denser
because the universe was smaller then.
The edge of the edge finally:
it's the beginning, the Big Bang.
The spear, Lucretius, thrown beyond space?
You could throw a spear
beyond the limit of the universe
but not where there's no more matter, and not even a spear.
        Or as the Greek said a javelin.
It's the heavens' end that is the beginning.

A telescope can look no further.
It could be calculated precisely, said Einstein,
the totality of its mass.
                    That gas of stars
                    and even more immense:
                    a gas of galaxies.
                        And
                        beyond?
                        Beyond the galaxies
                        what might there be?
Where did this come from and where is it going?

They flicker a little. Why do they flicker?
Because of our earth's atmosphere.
So to others our sun must flicker.
Gazing in this direction a love-struck man will say
that blue stars in the distance shiver.
And we among those stars.
Because of our atmosphere they appear to flicker.
With Venus's atmosphere you'd never see a star.
It took generations of them, stars I mean,
so that one day you'd be beautiful.
Ex-stars that were compressed into incredibly heavy
neutrons with a light iron membrane,
or like the star Cygnus X-1 an invisible thing
accompanies it with the mass of a hundred suns
which it seems was once a star and today a black hole.

                    The theory exists that you loved me.
                    My cousin Silvia stands by it.

And one day the planet will have disappeared
and ten thousand million years later,
there'll be others completely unaware of us
just as now, ten thousand million years before
                        others suffered, loved and dreamed
completely unknown to us.

Everything in the universe revolves.
So does the universe revolve too?
So what does it revolve around?
Everything in the universe revolves
and sphere is a being's desire
to be as small and as simple
as possible.

The humble planet like the manger in Bethlehem
cradle of life.
                The third planet,
in a Supergroup of galaxies 90% empty.

To understand the universe biologically.
The Kingdom of Heaven is biological.
Light which is energy and not matter.
The Big Bang created energy
and energy created matter.
Also invisible matter around you
and within you.
                From star atoms you . . .
And between you and the firmament there's no dividing line.

"Everything interpenetrates everything"
                                        says Bohm.
                Sighs are air and go into the air,
                but the oxygen molecule in your sigh
                did it cease to live as it left you?
Living and non-living matter are the same thing.
Just as there's also no emptiness, there is no empty space
and the entire universe is energy
which sometimes takes the form of matter.
Bohm again:
That each electron contains the entire cosmos.
Living and non-living matter are the same thing.
And when you, Claudia Argüello, are no longer alive
are you not alive?

There are atoms in the earth, in water and in the air
that later will be in a girl like Claudia
(as she was then)
and before being in her are they not alive?
The categories of body and soul are arbitrary,
and there is no dualism, Claudia.
                    Or a girl that is now like her,
as she used to be.
                    The ground you walk on is alive
                    and the air you breathe.
All in all.
And the interrelation of all with all according to Chardin
is increasingly greater.
Increasingly inadequate to think as individuals.

The girl you most loved and who did not love you
whether she likes it or not will be united with you
where everything is together in one point.
Fe/male reader, you may give these lines
to whoever it is that doesn't love you.

Like the rules of quantum mechanics.
So many years later: if perhaps she loved me.
She was my first love and it is as absurd now
as the rules of quantum mechanics.
The rules are that everything is probabilistic.
The love that never happened. Yet maybe it did.
Like the rules of quantum mechanics.

Proton and electron:
The closer they get the greater the attraction.
Like pink lips that draw close like two roses
and then the succulent mouths open
and one enters the other like copulation.
(Like a gentle blur of mouths I saw on the train
between Nuremberg and Munich.)

If we had 2×10^{1111} light years vision
instead of 2×10^{10} as we have
what would we see?

What waves are these that as they break form
that foam of galaxies that is the universe?
And that space be curved.
Curved like an apple.
Or like a woman's body,
the non-Euclidean geometry of woman?

The puddle in the street is very dirty
but in the puddle there is a clean sky
and in the sky an evergreen tree.
                    "Beauty is no accident of nature."
Beauty is functional, and its function is beauty.
Beauty is functional, it's to be seen.
          Tigers
are beautiful on the outside.
The viscera are monotonous.

The heron brings songs, say the Bora.
It inspires them, they mean (the Bora Indians).
Air was also for the trill and flight of birds.
The beauty of animals in light of which
Darwin's hypothesis of sexual selection
they say, is inadequate.
          "If nature were not beautiful . . ." (Poincaré)
The *Kosmos Kosmético* (beautiful) according to Justin.
And we are made to be satiated according to Justin,
St. Justin.
Although now the unjust oppress us.
          "If God were with you, Justin,
          the unjust would not oppress you"
said the pagan.
Kosmético, despite neoliberalism.
Which is why Heisenberg has said

that the universe is made not of matter or energy
but of music.

Elemental particles with elemental consciousness.
Anaxagoras said that the heavens and the earth
are made of the same substances
and they almost killed him for it.

The metals in our body
—soft bodies with metals—
as we know, come from stars.
Which we don't see. They no longer even exist.
What happened to them? They collapsed
into oblivion. Into black holes.
Our soft bodies with metals
born from black holes and from oblivion.
        You who were young and beautiful,
        once inspired epigrams
        and like my old age are old,
        look at the stars:
among them also there are stars now old.
Others that died. Or lived a few years,
a few hundreds of millions of years.

What if the next step is from man to robot . . .
—an obedient robot without capacity to sin—
and God has wanted a Kingdom of Heaven of robots.
No, says Faus, the Kingdom of Heaven won't be fascist.
Nor God saying:
"We lost. The socialist camp is no more.
We also lost the Sandinista elections.
Let's start again at the beginning. Let's change systems.
Let's leave this dumbass solar system."

Evil is because God made man free.
Because creation wasn't fascist.
He doesn't want the extinction

of a single one of his inhabited planets.
And the solar system is for the good and the evil.

But it's not true he created his creation
never to intervene again. I swear it's not.

If we have free will
doesn't God?
Between the ignorance of the atheist and the certainty of the idolater.
Creator. But creator of what?
Creator of creations. And in history
creator of creators. And so he can't do everything:
a circle squared.
                    Or worse still a Pentagon.
Atkins postulates a nonexistent creator,
but at the cost of a creation so simple
it's almost nonexistent.
(Where every complexity is apparent.)

An observer from one reference point
sees differently than another from another reference point.

A God who is love cannot be static
nor complete.
Beyond the ends of space which is the beginning of time.
Or according to Augustine outside of space-time.
Galaxies moving away from us
and all moving away from each other with no
center from which the galaxies are moving away.

Everything in the universe has cause.
            The succulent cactuses in the desert
            are thorny to defend their water.
                    So doesn't the universe have a cause?
Apples are tasty merely
to scatter the apple seeds
and the apple seeds merely

to produce tasty apples.
The theory now that our bodies come from comets
(our bodies 70% water,
and blood the wettest, almost all water)
from icy tails of comets that fell out of the sky.
The moon's orbit had to do
with falling apples.
And apples fall but the moon neither falls nor goes away.
The designer mind of the universe, says Sir J. Jeans
has something in common with our minds.
And Bohm sees intentionality in nature.

       Electrons do not exist but
       "have a tendency to exist."
               And we are composed of them!
Also every electron is the same as another electron
and it's the same as saying they're the same
or different.
      "We don't know whether physics describes physical things."

       Limited in the cosmos
        by the limits of language.
"An eccentric element in the physical world"
(particles)
     says Davies.
World of potentialities or possibilities
and not of things or facts.

      Scientists and mystics say it.

If the color is not in things,
nor sound, nor what we touch when we touch them,
but in us,
do things exist? and what are they like?
To Poincaré
a reality completely independent of the mind
is impossible, and if it were, what good is it to us?

And the possibility that there are infinite universes
though we are never able to observe them,
nor know where they are,
because our "where" is meaningless,
never able to communicate with them
nor know whether in reality they exist.

That we may, in principle,
travel back in time
as happens in science fiction,
and there be able to choose not to be born
as perhaps you did in innumerable universes
in which you were not born.
And I could choose never to have known you
but wouldn't do so.

If the theory is correct
everything possible is real somewhere.
Another theory is of a unique universe where everything is chance.
                    Those monkeys with typewriters
                    eternally typing Shakespeare.
And the new theory of the neo-realists:
that the universe is composed of ordinary things.

Computers have been made with beach sand.
Silicon is the main component of sand.
Sand of my sandcastles,
                    of a name written in the sand in Poneloya,
            of the imprint of two bodies in the sand,
a single wave wiped them out, leaving only the sand again.
Quasars the size of this solar system
but brighter than a trillion suns
and sometimes more than one hundred thousand galaxies, and a billionth
of a billionth of the diameter of the nucleus of an atom,
have been observed and calculated with this sand from the beach.
Sand upon which the galaxy-like foam from a wave
that is mere voluble probabilities fades away.

How many times from the sand have we gazed at the stars?
            The stars from which we come. Let's consider
the evolution of a star until it becomes a girl.
                  Entropy is anti-evolution
                  and at the end of the day does not exist.
            Evolution and transcendence:
                                    There's no difference.
The cosmos an as-yet unfinished process
and life is an interval in that process.
An earth that longs to be joined to heaven
and a God who is not merely ontological functions.
From the Big Bang to the Kingdom of Heaven.

Life on every favorable planet.
And universes wherever they may be favorable?
Prigogine postulates it.
A creator not of one but of multiple universes.
Infinite universes with a unique infinite God?
Parallel universes with exact copies of oneself
where you couldn't tell whether you are in one or the other.
Or perhaps one within the same space as the other.
Schrödinger's cat dead in one universe and alive in another.
And where quantum theory's contradictions are reconciled.

There's a need for new scientific metaphors.
Against pure mechanistics quantum mechanics means
that an electron has free will.
And also for new poetic metaphors.
            "Now there's a kind of intelligence in the electron."
On this still warm planet
and where fire burns within   (take a look at the Masaya volcano)
hotter than the surface of the sun.
            New Man and New Woman are
            a new biological event.
Bodies are elemental particles and fields of energy
yet souls do not exist alone
but only as something greater.

All matter is united according to Bohm.
So won't souls be even more so?
The boy and girl on a corner,
outside the pharmacy, and amid the honking of the taxis
he asked: "So what's your name?"
In Madrid, under the neon of the Mary Pharmacy:
          "What's your name?"
Every meeting of two unites the universe.
I'd gone by train from Nuremberg to Munich
where I read from *Cosmic Canticle* with quotations from Bohm included
and the Institute of Astrophysics invited me to chat with them
and we talked about physics and mysticism; extraterrestrials: one
said they don't exist; another denied Big Bang. With coffee and biscuits.
Another, that time does not exist, and another:
why say universe, as though it were only one
and not pluriverse?

[J. L.]

The stars you see
are in your retina, dear girl.
In the firmament of your eyes.
And if I look at the grass, the mountains,
as if they were outside
I don't see anything outside
but its image in my pupil.
And if I look at you as though outside
(talking now in this restaurant)
I see you only in my pupil.
And touching you, were I to touch you,
wouldn't be touching your skin
but mine, the vibrations in my brain.
It's not that you don't exist outside
dear friend, that you're not real
but your reality within me is an illusion.

So while we talk in this restaurant,
at the foot of the Alps, on a hill
a Disney castle.
Village bells singing in iron.
I say again that when I look at a person
his image is within me,
not outside where the person is.
And if I look three-dimensional in a mirror
it's only my flat image at the back
in the silvered depths of the mirror.
          So does objective reality not exist,
          a stone, a taxi, a mirror,
          or does it not exist as we believe it exists
          and it's true what mystics say
          that all reality is illusory?
Is what we call the real world mental?
In other words:
          what is the non-mental reality?
Is it world until it enters the senses?
Or perhaps consciousness and physical reality

are two manifestations of one and the same thing.
                    Does the world outside exist?
                    The world outside exists.
                    If the traffic light is red
                    it's red for everyone.
                              It's objective.
Borges's birds pass swiftly through the sky,
the theological birds whose number we never knew
but there has to be (he says) a mind that knows.
                    In this world of regular irregularity . . .
M is finite and it can be calculated precisely
according to Einstein (M is the mass of the universe)
and Eddington managed to calculate it in grams.
And I was traveling with Nicanor Parra on a bus in India
to the Taj Mahal, and he told me of the physicist who calculated
the exact number of atoms in the universe
and he said: let he who does not believe count them.

As I was saying before,
to see a rock
is not to see a rock
but the light the rock reflects.
Just as touching a woman
is merely having in your fingers
sensations of a woman's body.
What is outside of us is spectral.
Reality is organized in our mind.
                    If not, let quantum physics explain.
                    But no less real because it is mental.
Idealism and materialism are the same.
There is no matter without a mind to observe it
and without matter there is no brain with a mind
and much less an evolution of the mind.
              "Without matter there is nothing that can be seen,
              without observer there would be no universe."

A universe with no one to observe it,

wouldn't that be the same as one that doesn't exist?
And if everything is both objective and subjective?
No difference between reality and the mind?
Wave and particle are incompatible
and both are characteristic of matter.
We're made of incompatible matter.
In a universe the greater part of which
is intergalactic emptiness.
And a universe where
"the characteristic of atoms is their emptiness."

Materialist we are
yet it so happened that matter wasn't solid
but interactions of fields of energy.
The wave is not a real wave but of probabilities.
                    Quantum mechanics, about which
                    Feynman says, no one understands.
We cannot observe naked reality,
the observation is part of what's observed.
Subject and object: who can separate them for us?
The apple is on the table and in the mind.
        And the woman who cuts the apple?
Well yes, this matter of ours in which
        "an electron not observed is unreal."
In which
        "a prerequisite of reality is observing it."
And also the mind as a property of matter.
Materialism? When we don't even know what matter is.
And consciousness is not in the body's atoms
since the atoms last such a short time in the body.
I was twenty once.
        When forever appears in the equation
it is the black hole.
Black hole in which time stands still
and space extends to infinity.

Energy and electricity are realities

and we don't know what they are.
The electromagnetic field says Feynman
more difficult to imagine than the invisible angels.
Waves and particles are metaphors, says Gribbin.
And Heisenberg says we can't
      "talk about atoms in everyday language."
Matter then like a mathematical abstraction?
Carmen was her name
         and she was no mathematical abstraction in those days.
They've discovered that electrons have sex.
At the heart of the atom a nuptial chamber.
      "Unity is plural with a minimum of two."
And particles like different musical notes?
      The analogy is good says Witten.
(Musical notes.)
Rhythm is duality. One alone would be monotonous.
Just as one cannot make oneself happy oneself.

The universe increasingly less machine and more soul.
Matter is almost in its entirety empty space,
we said, but there's no space so empty
that it isn't teeming with ephemeral and spectral particles.
The emptiness is not nothingness rather it is full of energy
apparently without permanent particles
      —and our bodies are full of emptiness!
The solid billiard balls
have become soft and confused probabilities.
Emptiness no longer vacuous but rather alive and palpitating
"We call them particles for want of a better name.
What they are in reality, we don't know."
The thing is complicated. According to Heisenberg, mathematics
does not represent the action of elemental particles,
but rather our knowledge of this action.
Mere matter then turned out to be merely absurd quarks
thus called after an absurd joke in Finnegans Wake.

The theory that solid matter dissolves

in excitations of invisible fields of energy
and a distinction no longer exists between material substance
and emptiness (that is, apparently empty space).
     And the universe is almost imaginary
     or rather is pure information.
An intangible sub-atomic particle but
from which such tangible matter is made.
The "probability wave" half Aristotelian,
     a kind of physical reality
     between reality and possibility.
Again as I was saying before:
that non-observed reality is not real.
And an object has no attributes if nobody sees it
(von Neumann).
And that all vision of the eye is optical illusion,
dear girl.

     "Even the color of steak isn't real."

Just as the electron doesn't exist if it's not observed.
Matter is real or unreal, as you wish.
     Quanta, a schizophrenic cosmos.
   That matter is particles is metaphor
and that they are waves, metaphor too.
And with atoms, Bohr says, language
can only be used as in poetry.

Ah, the atom which is almost entirely empty space
and all things are made of atoms,
     including you and I.
          Quantum world doesn't exist said Bohr
          merely a quantum description of the world.
And:
"Physics is not for understanding nature,
just what we say about nature."

Indetermination at the heart of matter.

The quantum principle already in Parmenides.
And to Bohm the entire universe is a hologram.
And consciousness a more subtle form of matter.

Particle which is, one way or another,
according to whether it's observed or not.
My decision about how to observe an electron
changes the electron.
        An electron is not objective.
  Because an electron cannot be observed
  without increasing the electron's energy
  so we don't know what the electron was like.
           But virtual particles
           that can never be observed:
           how do they really exist
           as virtual particles?
And the atoms which are made of particles
which are not made of anything material,
without substance, only dance of energy,
movement with no one moving,
only dance with no dancers.
"You can enjoy the delights of quantum theory
so long as you don't try to understand it."

And then Bohm's point:
                "everything interpenetrated with everything."
  Antigravity has never been observed.
To Newton: the spirit, investigable through physics.
Democritus held that the soul had atoms (special atoms).
Electrons of my body that have been in the wind,
in the sea, trees, animals,
             and even in other galaxies.
      That's what binds us all in brotherhood.
A destiny confined to one planet alone?

That time elapses at different speeds.
And the distance between two faraway places is zero

because the difference is in time nothing more!
What demented geometry is that
in which space is curved?
Curve of nothing upon nothing
with no direction in which to curve.
(Now schoolchildren understand it.)

The curve's not space but space-time
and no thing is curved.
The reality of modern physicists
is fundamentally alien to the human mind, says Davies.

Complexity of the brain and simplicity of the mind.
And between the complex and the simple
where are memories stored?
Memories, alas, and oblivion.
Our life and time in opposite directions
like a train racing in a tunnel
and the lights racing backwards.

When you have no answer, look at the stars,
(the stars that are in your retina).
It's not that they answer. They ask questions too
looking at us, inhabitants of a star.
We all will be the answer, them and us,
because we all are the sadness.
Perhaps the fact there're so many of us in the galaxies
will be the salvation.

After Einstein it was demonstrated
that one grows older more slowly
as one moves forward faster.
So isn't an infinite velocity
a time without old age?
To Einstein space is real
and time imaginary, or vice versa.
So what if there's a spiritual space-time

concealed in elemental particles
and that science cannot detect?
What if the resurrection of the bodies
will be of those elemental particles
that were also in other bodies,
elemental particles beyond which
nothing else exists anymore, but God alone?
All the cells in our body
have the same chromosomes, whether
in the eye, the heart, the liver
so if the particles of the chromosomes
are each and every one the same particle,
the whole cosmos is like a single chromosome?
So we better understand, albeit vaguely, Carmen,
the sweet dogma of the resurrection of your flesh.
The you within you
your deepest you,
conscious of its consciousness,
reflection of mirror in mirror
(in other words infinite mirrors)
is what doesn't die. But I don't want
to go on living after death
merely as pure information.
The soul merely information?
As Bohm maintains
                              (and not just Bohm)
everything is of a piece although we see it in parts.
But the separations felt as valid.
            A trapeze in my childhood swinging
            in an arbor at my aunt Antonina's,
            very faded now the trapeze and garden . . .
                        Everything is connected with everything,
                        even sub-atomic particles
                        separated by billions of years.
From quasars to a tiny birthday candle.
What Bohm has called "non local."
Nothing is anywhere.

At the sub-atomic level everything together everywhere.
Heaven and earth have been separated since Aristotle
and for that reason the moon never fell.
Until Newton discovered that we were the same
heaven and earth, and for that reason the moon never fell.
The universal implication of the falling apple.
If the apple doesn't fall it's because everything falls on everything.
And only on the planet do up and down exist.
On the scale of the universe it makes no difference
if we say a year or a thousand years. And a now distant garden.
     The red shift
Space expands, not the galaxies. But
into what does space expand? into another space?
The star that collapses in on itself
because of its density and disappears
—where does it go to?
     Oh Bohm, may your theory be true.

The mystery we carry inside of the mind.
Is the red apple the same for you as for me?
It was the same for Adam as for Eve,
although their neurons were different
                (Newton's too).
Apples rot and so do neurons
but something that doesn't die emerges like a butterfly
from the complexity of the brain and the simplicity of the mind,
     from what Teresi called our 3-pound universe.

[J. L.]

Lover and beloved. The lover
gazes from her bedroom at the moon rising.
A motorcycle accelerating in the street.
            The beloved in no hurry to come to bed.

I was born for an extremist love.
Perhaps that's why we understand each other.
            You're an even greater extremist!
And I still hardly know you.

The surest guarantee that it's true
and not an invention of mine
                    is that you give me no pleasure.
Mysterious beloved from whom I get no pleasure,
        all I want is to be with you!

You leave and come back,
inconstant *sparrowe*,
then once again you leave.

What good is it to me that the moon is beautiful
if I am without you?
I don't even want to see it over the lake.
It will be for others.
The mysterious sounds of the night.
If they are without you.

A cruel invisible glass separates us.
            Infinite abyss between the two of us
and wanting to embrace you.
                    And perhaps embracing you.
                            Or think I'm embracing you.

This park in Madrid . . . Take a look
my immaterial lover at those bodies kissing one another.
If you love me
and I love you

What is it then that does not unite us
in the universe?
As though we were in parallel universes.

If they could hear what I say to you at times
they'd be scandalized. Really, what blasphemies!
But you understand my reasons.
                    And besides I'm teasing.
And they're things that people in love say to each other in bed.

I ask
is it normal for you to love me so much?
I ask
what must the beauty you love be like?
what must my eyes be like that you see?
the face that enchants you?

I have a secret love
that no-one sees.
We keep it so secret
they see only me.

Electricity is a manner of speaking.
              Like repels and opposite attracts.
Like male and female. But
positive and *negative* is a manner of speaking.
                I love you as opposite,
                and it's not a manner of speaking.
The fact that everything in the universe is male and female
(in homosexual relations too in their way)
the fact that everything is male and female, is for me confirmation
                that celibacy is a marriage.

Who holds in himself the reason for his existence,
cause of all and caused by no-one . . .
"Well, own up now: is that your friend?"
Yes. I imagine myself like two who wander off from the group

and spend the entire outing chatting on their own,
the waves breaking below, the tiger-striped water,
the slow setting of the sun on the Pacific.

Without a special identity
           nor solicitous of human beings,
I read in a scientist's work.
Identity, I don't know;
but he cares for every one of my electrons.
Is present within all of my electrons.

Not in the slightest affected by the universe's existence
according to the Scholastics.
                         That's not right?

So what's going on between you and me?
Could it perhaps be you love me
but I don't love myself?
That I don't love myself maybe so
but that doesn't impede our union
if you really love me and I love you.

He must be infinite the one I love
but I'm insensible to his infinite loves
with infinite lovers
rather my beloved is mine alone.
Infinite he is but infinitely mine.
Concerning love God isn't one.
There are infinite Beloveds, one for everyone.
I know. I have my own.
I know him, and he knows me
infinitely.

When I was in love with her it was like that,
those evenings in Tacubaya with a cigarette,
thinking of her, she in her twilit Granada,
me with no other reality than my cigarette

and the sparks of the streetcars on the electric cables
criss-crossing above that Tacubaya street
and the many neon lights in the Mexican night
that merely cast more light on my separation.
No, the love was unreal. It's not a good comparison.

They say you're a process and not a person.
To me, process or not process, it's personal.
When you fell into my nets I don't know.
Since I was a youngster playing baseball?
Or since the Pleistocene, or earlier?
Was it gradual or sudden?
Maybe you tell me: always.

You took everything from me,
so give me all of you then.

I'm intrigued to know what it was you liked about me.
Perhaps a soul with sad eyes.
And a flavor yet to be tasted by anyone.

It would appear now that you don't love me.
Worse still, that you don't even exist.
Even if you didn't exist I love you
and could love you without you loving me.
But you are, and I love the one who loves me.

Even if you don't come to me tonight
my heart has been left open for you.
In case you came. If you don't come
it will be open in any case to you
and nobody else.

If we could conceive of the infinite
we'd know how much he loves us.
But since the infinite to us is the same as 0
   we feel zero

(which is what is attained in the highest prayer).
Better united to you whom I don't feel,
of whom I really feel nothing at all
than to any other love I might really feel.
Beloved, the meadows are in flower.
Happy the love that's taken hold of me, which is
        alas! Love = 0.

Yesterday I felt your face deeper inside than my eyes
and today light years away from me as in another galaxy.
        Ernesto's sad gazes for you
        —have you seen them?
Me, a master of solitudes.

I'm not mercenary in this love.
I want love, not saccharine sentimentalities.
It could be completely barren. (I can take it.)
For I've been an intimate of sadness for so long.

If of nothing,
if it's a matter of feeling nothing,
mine's a perfect love.
If it's a matter of feeling nothing.
    And in truth it is a matter.

Loving the one who has so much beauty
that we don't see it.
The light of his face as though it were ultraviolet.

Don't allow me to want it, for this to happen:
to desire you and no longer be able to see you ever again.
You'll lose a great deal too.
But of the two of us I lose more than you.

They said to Giaconda Belli in that bar
that she could train me in eroticism
and she said that she could train me a great deal.

I said nothing. Today I thought
there's an eroticism free of the senses, for very few,
        in which I'm an expert.

    There is a cooing among the leaves
    —the other cooing can't be heard—
    as though it were inside me
    awaiting yours.
To go on loving you while I'm alive
expecting nothing from this love
as though you didn't exist
and for the love to persist,
my Love, is this not love indeed?
       Moan moan moan
moan moan moan moan moan
repeated moaning is the cooing
          if you want me to come, I will,
          if you want me to come, I will.

    It's hard,
but I make no complaint of bodiless love
which has been my lot.
You wanted me for yourself alone.
And lonelier than now is not possible.

The tenderness with which they love
in parks or movie theaters or in bedrooms,
and what will our tenderness be like,
so tender that the senses do not feel it,
tenderness beyond tenderness, way beyond.

As a young man I considered myself
a champion in capacity to love
—and in reality I was one—now I'm one
             in matters of solitude.

Who was tireless in waiting

in the atrium of La Merced or on the corner
could wait a lifetime for you,
creator of that girl I loved.

The sea, a rose, a woman,
each thing speaks to us of God.
But a bikini-clad woman in the sea
tells us too that she is not God.
Every being is transparent, but
the transparency is nothing other
than a not being so the light may pass through.

Unite with me even though I cannot feel you, even
though my consciousness stays out in the cold.
My Lord and my God of my frustrations.
Let's at least make believe we are lovers.

Those who have arms without embraces.
           The medieval hermit who envied a rooster.
To ruffle a little hair at the very least,
followed by brush of some lips, brush of some skin,
love like a tidal wave the height of palm trees.
           My classmates laughed
when I called out to Father Otaño to come and see the sight
of two insects with their tails stuck together.
At another point in my life
I have envied not only my lost childhood but
insects.

Love, between the two of us, with no sex
but which is as though it were sex.
Not physiological, alas!, not bodily
but of which copulation is the fleeting image.

Like the impatient couple in the park waiting for nightfall.

Super-intellect of the universe

they have called you.
I simply call you:
                    my beloved.
With me you certainly played dice
and risked so much
and many times about to lose
yet you won.
But weren't the dice loaded?
                    Occasionally you overstepped the mark
                    with regard to my free will.
                              So great was your love
                              that you violated it.

One day I'll embrace you outside time
where everything happens at the same time.
                    Round and round on its axis,
                    day and night round and round,
                    and there's day and night because it spins around.
                    We know nothing of other planets
but on this one you've made it so we sleep
and reclining on your breast I have fallen asleep
while the airplanes come and go.

I hadn't a moment's prayer today.
Does that really mean we were less together?

I don't know where the real foliage ends
and where the water foliage begins.
                    These aquatic landscapes
                    where the water reflects everything
                    and which so enchant us
                    are the reflection of your face
                    which is why they enchant us so.

That mysterious union riding the car
through Managua streets, highways,
which is so tender, and which nobody notices.

Free will throughout the galaxies.
Terror of the universe free will.
Capable of losing you, my love, should I so wish.

In the hammock I felt you were telling me
I didn't choose you because you were a saint
or with the makings of a future saint
saints I've had too many
                    I chose you for a change.

And me who'd so often been in love.
                    Were you jealous?

The tenderness of certain words such as
"the two of us."
            I stroll alone among the kisses.
                    From my solitudes I come
                    to my solitudes may I never return.
I felt that eternity
would be the two of us together.
God loves me as though I were God.
One day I'll be an expert lovemaker
in your bed, between the sheets.
            Sex of God.

The guy who had more loves than all his buddies,
the guy who loved most in his whole generation,
loving now such a transcendent type,
not to say a non-existent character.
Look what's become of you, Ernesto.

You could inspire better poetry if you wished
in verses that will circulate perhaps throughout Spanish America
and will perhaps arouse in others who read them
a greater love than the love the poet had for you.

"It knows not how it knows" says St. Teresa.

Whether it's prayer or isn't prayer, what does it matter.
My soul is simply on its back looking up
waiting for you to leap on me.

To love a love that never ages
and to love him without me ever aging.
So beautiful the visible, I know that,
but far more beautiful the invisible
I know of no other fucking way to call it
that, that thing which is where you make love.

My consolation is remembering what you did to me that 2nd of June.
Now you're as far from me as Ileana—remember?—
and the Andromeda Galaxy.
When Ileana on Candelaria Street was more distant from me
than the Andromeda Galaxy.
My consolation is remembering what you did to me that 2nd of June
37 years ago.

Once again you appear like music, like light,
music without sound waves, light without photons.
Caress without touch, only pure caress.
          The one who invented sex
          —shouldn't he know how to make love?

How shall I describe
the joy of being in love?
It's having no longer a lonely heart,
that empty dwelling,
now occupied by the one you love.
          It's being two where once one.

The infinite and I,
been together for quite some time,
and on intimate terms, isn't that so?
When even saying I love you seems superfluous.
Words are many and they say little.

Better silence. To gaze on you with mute soul
eyes moist like a dog's.

Truth is
I made the first move.
Not that I loved you first, rather
that even before I ever loved you, feeling so defeated
on the 2nd of June I declared my unconditional surrender.
                    That's how it all began.

"Prayer of repose," then "union" . . .
St. Teresa has her vade mecum.
Bend your rules for me.
Though ours may be a clandestine, illicit affair.

The two of us are alone
in my small white cottage by the lake.
Against the dark green foliage
the heron's flight is a brilliant white
but it leaves the island and enters the sunlight
and disappears from sight.
The two of us are alone
though only one can be seen.

Ephemeral it was, super-ephemeral
that which I renounced,
but it wasn't for the non-ephemeral,
shall I tell you the truth?
rather it was for what *is not*.
                    But, but
I prefer to bemoan your absence, and
your not being here, your—I don't know—your not being.
Not that I'm a great one for absences,
shall I tell you the truth?
no other presence is better.

Last night I dreamed of a coitus, a realistic dream, hyper-realistic.

You torment me with the flesh
               so that I'll love you more
               but not in the flesh.

That midday of the 2nd of June in '56
when you entered me and spoke to me
               I'd yet to fall in love.

The river an almost black green
except where the sky is reflected
but it's reflected in a black mirror.
               I'm not in communion with that.
          Beloved, let's make love.
I don't know what they mean by "giving glory to God." Love yes.
To me glory is
having God in my bed or in the hammock.
                         Let's give pleasure to each other.
          The stone curlews are in flight.
Let's give pleasure to each other, beloved.

You're closer to me than I am.
Which is why you seem so distant.
               I imagine you must feel great pity for me.
What will that day be like when you say Ernesto?

Be jealous no more.
Mirrors of physical beauty
will never again deceive me.

My happiness was paltry. The loneliness is absolute.
I who was once such a lovesick romantic:
to embrace without arms, to love without emotions.
               It would be sweet to cry but it's just rhetoric.
Maybe the romantic and lovesick appealed to you.
               One in a hundred thousand you chose me.
The epigrams and girls were left behind.

I've been gelded,
not in Somoza's jails
but for the Kingdom (Mt. 19:12).

Joaquín Pasos in that bar
after having been in a room with his girl
to Juan Aburto:
        "Poet, God's in women's cunts."
    According to the catechism he's everywhere.
    But not the same presence everywhere.

And:
    Eunuchs. Out of love for the Kingdom of Heaven.
        That's no joke either.

My atoms,
which are mine only for a short while,
since others will follow,
tell my beloved I'll be his
once I am stripped of all atoms.

Out of love for the Kingdom of Heaven.
Origen did it literally.

Sometimes loveless, most of the time, or so it seems,
or the lonely love of myself, poor me,
in a universe swarming with so many others. Or perhaps
not, not the lonely love of me alone, but subtly,
so it's not even felt, another, as close as I am to me.

To hold each other in our arms,
both entering the other's embrace.
How different to feel you inside me
than to feel my aloneness inside me,
that's to say, empty.
        Could it be that aloneness is your embrace
        and your kisses mere thirsting?

I seem to hear you saying you can never get enough of me.
Me who was once such a fine connoisseur of heartaches.

I get goose bumps when I think
how you will say it
when you say my name.

And what you have in mind for me for later on.

That night on Vancouver Island
I opened the small motel window
and seeing the stars
I almost cried.
There were so many that night
and in each of them you were sending me a kiss.

      You fell in love with me.
"Call it God if you like"
says a science book.
I don't care whether I do
or don't call you that
but I love you.
      Even if you didn't love me I love you.

To take a very deep sigh
and to sigh again.
   To think:
      What if I were to hear you sigh!

I've been very passionate.
The story of my life has been a story of love.
     Of love? Of loneliness!
Of loneliness and love.
        Of loneliness.
   Sexually
very passionate.

Behold your lover is naked.
Will she put on her robe once again?

Or as though forgetful of creation
so as to be with me. To play.
I was flying over the Amazon, the labyrinth of waters,
rivers branching off as far as the horizon. Borges
was never here but must have seen it in his blind and sleepless nights.
The light aircraft below the clouds, almost touching the rivers.
I with no sense of you as creator of all this.
I'd be afraid of you. I sense you
as someone joined to me, as equals.
In order to love me you must be my size.
                        With such a huge difference
                        how could I love you?

Time, I hate you. Even though I wouldn't exist without you.
And in your passing I'll die although in your passing I was born.
Like St. Francis of Borgia I want now
to love someone whom time doesn't touch
and for us to rent a room where night never ends
nor the neon signs go out one by one.

Supposing millions of planets with consciousness
in millions of galaxies, as is the case,
it surprises me that there being so many loves in all of them
you should have such a special relationship as this with me, as
for example in the Denver airport changing planes
I apparently alone amid the hubbub of passengers:
we were sitting together like two sweethearts.

I who have had the bad luck
that God should have fallen in love with me.
I've been excluded from the erotic game.
Others in those games will laugh at me.
            At the time of my boundless love
            in Granada were you jealous?

My sexual desires have been and are
merely analogies of my love for you.
I believe my sexual desires please you.

If as some believe there are infinite universes
mustn't there be an infinite number of God, one for each universe?
Or a single infinite one for the infinite universes?
What do I care. I've made a bed for him among the flowers
that transcend the equations and mathematics.
I myself am the bed.

I wouldn't be a believer had I not
already tasted your pleasure.
        The one who invented sexual pleasure,
        none other than he.
Have you come again to torment me,
to stir my desires?
Were you to enter.
Not just breast against breast,
as you have done, but were you also to enter.
Being together is not the same as being the same.

"I have no-one else" I've told him
and said so over and over again.
And I heard him saying inside me
not with words exactly
or yes in a confusion of precise
words, he was saying inside me
or from the depths of the universe:
"And I've no-one else but you."

Not being able to pray doesn't bother me.
        Together the infinite and I, me
        not feeling the least thing.
Just as if God didn't exist.
Simply nothing. Can there be
any greater intimacy as far as the infinite goes?

Our relations . . .
This symbiosis that we are.
You know what I was after:
beauty that doesn't grow fat,
love that doesn't turn bourgeois.
                On the other hand you:
    you wanted someone to love
    which is why I was made.
I did nothing to win your heart.
My renunciations
are still gushing blood.

To be able to settle for natural beauty
and no longer pursue you, the immaterial one;
natural beauty; if even a naked woman
could satisfy me, and I no longer chased you inconsolably!

And Merton: his last warning
in the *Guest House* before admitting me to the cloister:
"The life of a monk is
a semi-ecstasy and forty years of aridity."
        It didn't frighten me.

When that midday on June 2nd, a Saturday,
Somoza García in a flash of lightning sped along Roosevelt Avenue
all horns blaring to ward off the traffic,
in that very instant, just like his triumphant motorcade
you just as triumphant suddenly entered me
and my poor defenseless soul wanting to cover its private parts.
            It was almost rape,
            but with consent,
            how could it be otherwise,
            and that invasion of pleasure
            until almost dying,
            and saying: that's enough
            you're killing me.
                So much pleasure that produces so much pain.

Like a kind of penetration.

I pray arid prayer
in the hotel where they've put me
        among glass skyscrapers
                quadrangular terraced hulks
the sunset reflected in the panes of glass
or other glass skyscrapers reflected
with the sky behind them also reflected
but the skyscrapers brighter than the sky
        with their luminous black plate glass
                and already some with lights on inside,
reflecting other panes of glass opposite black and shining
                and those lit up,
        reflections of reflections these hulks
and in this prayer I pray nothing, no
                words, ideas nor emotions,
its only purpose:
that it send up to you this prayer in the cold symmetry
        of nothings upon nothings reflecting nothings
                on 50th St. & Park Ave.

[J. L.]

What's in a star? We are.
All the elements of our body and of the planet
were once in the belly of a star.
      We are stardust.
15,000,000,000 years ago we were a mass
of hydrogen floating in space, turning slowly, dancing.
      And the gas condensed more and more
      gaining increasingly more mass
      and mass became star and began to shine.
As they condensed they grew hot and bright.
Gravitation produced thermal energy: light and heat.
That is to say love.
          Stars were born, grew, and died.
And the galaxy was taking the shape of a flower
the way it looks now on a starry night.
Our flesh and our bones come from other stars
and perhaps even from other galaxies,
we are universal,
and after death we will help to form other stars
and other galaxies.
      We come from the stars, and to them we shall return.

[J. C.]

JONATHAN COHEN (1949–), U.S. poet, translator, essayist, and scholar of inter-American literature, is the author of the translations of Ernesto Cardenal's *With Walker in Nicaragua and Other Early Poems* and *From Nicaragua, With Love: Poems*, winner of the Robert Payne Award of the Translation Center at Columbia University, plus work by poets Enrique Lihn, Pedro Mir, and Roque Dalton. He has been translating Cardenal since 1970.

MIREYA JAIMES-FREYRE (1921–), Bolivian-born U.S. poet (Xalmán group) and professor emerita of Latin American literature at the University of California, Santa Barbara, is the author of critical works on Spanish modernism and on Bolivian *modernista* poet Ricardo Jaimes Freyre.

JOHN LYONS (1950–), Irish poet, translator, teacher, and musician, who currently resides in Brazil, is the author of translations of poetry by Ernesto Cardenal, notably his *Cosmic Canticle* and *The Doubtful Strait*, and more recently a Spanish translation of Harold Pinter's poetry.

THOMAS MERTON (1915–1968), U.S. Roman Catholic monk (Trappist), and also poet, translator, religious writer, and essayist, is the author of translations of poetry by Nicanor Parra and Pablo Antonio Cuadra, as well as prose works from French, Latin, and classic Greek.

ROBERT PRING-MILL (1924–2005), English translator and professor of Hispanic literatures at Oxford University, is the author of critical works on Ernesto Cardenal, Pablo Neruda, and other Latin American poets, plus the translation of Cardenal's *Marilyn Monroe and Other Poems*.

KENNETH REXROTH (1905–1982), U.S. poet, translator, playwright, essayist, and co-founder, with Allen Ginsberg and Lawrence Ferlinghetti, of the San Francisco Poetry Center, is the author of translations of Chinese, Japanese, classic Greek, and Spanish-language poetry.

DONALD D. WALSH (1903–1980), U.S. teacher of French and Spanish at the Choate School, is the translator of poetry by Pablo Neruda, Pedro Mir, Angel González, and Angel Cuadra, as well as prose works, including Ernesto Cardenal's *In Cuba* and *The Gospel in Solentiname*.